L. L. Bean Fly Fishing for Bass Handbook

Written and Illustrated by
DAVE WHITLOCK

NICK LYONS BOOKS

Printed in the United States of America

10 9 8 7 6 5 4 3 2 1

Library of Congress Cataloging-in-Publication Data

Whitlock, Dave.
 L. L. Bean fly fishing for bass handbook.

 Bibliography: p.
 1. Bass fishing. 2. Fly fishing. I. Title.
II. Title: LL Bean fly fishing for bass handbook.
SH681.W47 1988   799.1'758   88-5217
ISBN 0-941130-76-2 (pbk.)

This handbook is dedicated to
JOAN WHITLOCK, NICK LYONS, PAUL LEONARD, JR.,
and the L. L. BEAN COMPANY.
Their special help and support on this project
has been invaluable to me

Contents

INTRODUCTION

Fly fishing for bass may well be the most exciting, pleasurable, and consistently rewarding method of fishing that exists today in North America. Bass are by a wide margin our most popular freshwater gamefish. They are abundant, widely distributed, and self-sustaining. They will attack an enormous range of artificial lures, especially if these lures represent their natural foods or compete for their food or territory. Their forage areas, their aggressive attack on a fly—especially surface flies—and their leaping, dogged fight never cease to thrill anglers. Bass are terrific fun on a fly rod!

Though fly fishing for bass is not new, fly fishing was usually associated with trout, salmon, and similar cold-water fish. This was mainly because such fish were the chief gamefish in Europe and the British Isles; as sport-fishing developed in North America, an inherited narrow-mindedness kept bass from becoming a popular fly-rod quarry.

Most fly fishers here were influenced by this traditional focus on trout, and most fly-fishing literature and teaching has always been lopsided toward trout and salmon, too.

Traditionalist fly fishers saw trout as a beautiful, delicate, highly intelligent, sophisticated fish living in pure, crystal-clear streams. They saw bass as coarse, dark, moody, gluttonous, and foolish, living in murky, stagnant swamps somewhere down South. Both images are true for both fish!

But they're not the whole story.

Bass do live in some pretty terrible-looking areas and sometimes are so gullible as to seem stupid; but they did not get to be our most popular gamefish by those qualifications. Bass also live in waters high and low that are as pristine as any that trout inhabit. Most bass fisheries—unlike a lot of marginal trout waters—need never be stocked by man to maintain good fishing. When you catch a bass, it's nearly always a wild fish.

Living in Oklahoma, in nearly troutless country, as a boy I brainwashed myself into thinking that bass were simply not a fish worth being pursued and caught on a fly rod. It wasn't that fly fishing for bass hadn't been explored. Dr. James Henshall, Jason Lucas, Ted Trueblood, Joe Brooks, Ray Bergman, and many others had made fine contributions to the flies, tackle, and techniques of fly-rodding for bass. Unfortunately, their work had not persuaded large numbers of fly fishers to pursue bass aggressively—and enjoy doing so. I was one of the unconvinced. Though I did some fly fishing for bass when I was a boy, I chiefly used it to supplement other more practical methods such as baitcasting and spinning. In fact, I stopped fly fishing for bass entirely when spin-fishing was introduced to me in the late 1940s because I could present small lures better with this method and consistently caught more and larger bass in the streams and lakes of Arkansas, Oklahoma, Missouri, and Texas on spinning lures.

Like so many others, I associated the fly rod in the 1940s through 1960s with panfish in warm water and trout and salmon in cold. Then, eighteen years ago, I became a fishing professional and began to live and breathe fly fishing and fly tying.

It troubled me that I could not catch big bass year round on a fly rod. But why not? The standard argument was that the fly rod was just not strong enough to hook and land big bass . . . say a real mean largemouth of four to ten pounds. Yet fly fishers routinely caught Atlantic and king salmon up to forty or fifty pounds. And tarpon were caught up to 100 pounds. And even sailfish and marlin had been taken on a fly rod. Even though I'd had poor results casting bass flies and hooking large bass, I was not persuaded that it could not be done—especially since I regularly caught four to eight-pound bass on six or eight-pound-test spinning tackle.

Then three people influenced me greatly. My wife Joan repeatedly insisted that fly fishing for bass and panfish could be more fun than fishing for trout. Garvice "Porky" Loucks, one of my Oklahoma fly-fishing buddies, moved from Colorado to Oklahoma because he found fly-rodding for bass—after years of fly fishing for trout in the Rockies—to be far more exciting and challenging. His shift amazed me. How could that be?

The late Lew Jewett of 3M/Scientific Anglers was the third influence. Lew was a good friend and I very much wanted to help expand fly-line sales for him; I knew that if I could get bass fishermen more serious about fly fishing and fly fishers to switch-hit for bass that would really help.

So I started a comprehensive study of fly fishing for bass that has lasted for the past fifteen years. I began by leaving all my other bass tackle at home and fished only with flies and fly tackle—all day, each day, month after month, all year. That forced me to think, observe, and experiment each time out and it kept me thinking overtime when I was off the water. What I discovered was that fly fishing could be as effective as any other method for bass—*if specific flies, tackle, and methods* were used. A lot of the older methods and flies simply were not as efficient as they should be. Traditional trout and salmon fly fishing was almost entirely different from what was required to catch bass on flies. No wonder so many fly fishers and lure casters felt the fly rod was not equal to the job of catching big bass!

Once I discovered what the real problems were in catching big bass on flies, I solved most of them by studying and adapting the successful methods of the saltwater fly fishers and the spin and baitcasting bass fishermen.

My methods for successful bass fishing with fly tackle and flies are simple and highly productive. They will allow you to get a head start enjoying fly fishing for bass—and I promise you'll enjoy it as much or more than any other type of fly fishing. Also, my methods are not just applicable to large and smallmouth bass but to virtually all predator fish in cool, warm, or brackish water—and even to trophy trout. To simplify this handbook, I'll just use the word "bass" to describe all these fish.

Because bass and such other closely associated species as bluegill, crappie, perch, rock bass, white bass, stripers, pike, pickerel, muskie, and the like are so abundant in nearly every state, Mexico, and Canada, there is unlimited fly fishing at our doorsteps. Trout live farther from most cities; quality opportunities to fish for them are becoming scarcer and more expensive.

Bass, however, are probably less than an hour's drive from your home—which means a lot to those of us who need to relax by fly fishing every week.

This handbook, then, is written mainly for three groups of fishermen:

1. Bass fishermen who would enjoy catching bass more if they also fly fished;

2. Trout and salmon fly fishermen who would double their annual fishing pleasure—*and time on the water*—if they learned to fly fish for bass; and

3. Fly-fishing beginners, who will find bass and panfish perfect for their first efforts on the water because these fish, unlike trout, are nearly always available and willing to hit flies regardless of one's· skill level.

I hope this handbook will help all three groups. Fly-rodding for bass is lots of fun—and I want to share all I've learned about this exciting sport.

Dave Whitlock
December 1987

L. L. Bean
Fly Fishing
for Bass
Handbook

1
Bass Basics

Consistently successful fly fishing for bass is dependent upon how well you understand these fish. In particular, you must learn where bass live, how they survive and feed, and how the cycles of day and year affect their activities.

Bass comprise six or seven species and subspecies of the sunfish family *(Centrachidae)*. Of these, the largemouth and smallmouth bass are the most popular, abundant, and widely distributed. There is a northern species and a southern-Florida subspecies of largemouth, and the smallmouth has at least two groups—the northern and the midsouth Neosho smallmouth. A third bass, the spotted or Kentucky bass, though far less widely distributed, is important to fly fishermen; three small bass—the Suwannee, Guadalupe, and Redeye—which live in a narrow range, are not especially important.

Most of this handbook will refer to the largemouth and smallmouth bass. One or both species occur naturally or by introduction in all states except Alaska and parts of Canada and Mexico. The other bass look like hybrids or crossbreeds of these two major species, though some are not; since they fall between the main basses in many of their habits, successful methods, flies, and tackle for the major two often work well for the others.

It's a good bet you'll find bass in nearly any stream or lake that is not specifically inhabited by trout. Though bass, like all fish, are cold-blooded (unlike birds and mammals they cannot regulate or maintain their body temperatures), they have a 10° to 20°F higher range of metabolic activity than trout. Bass can tolerate a wide range of different water environments. They can endure water temperatures ranging from the low 30's to 90°F. But bass will not flourish if the local water tem-

Two lovely and characteristic specimens of largemouth (top) and smallmouth bass.

peratures are not in the 55° to 80°F range at least four or five months each year; ideally, six or more months of waters averaging 60° to 75° causes their metabolism to be most active and efficient.

Bass seek the most comfortable water temperatures throughout the year, especially if there is ample food, cover, and oxygen. Usually you'll find them in shallow water in the spring and early summer, moving deeper to keep cool as the summer sun heats the shallows. By early fall they're back in shallow water, where they stay until the cold water of late fall and winter makes them seek deeper water again, where they will be warmer and more secure when the cold makes them less active.

Catching bass on surface and subsurface flies becomes relatively difficult below 55°F and very difficult below 50°F. Curiously, the largemouth, which prefers warmer water, does remain active below 50°, whereas most smallmouth become dormant. Smallmouth seem better adapted to the cooler range of 55° to 75°, whereas largemouth prefer temperatures of 60° to 80°. Each adapts well when stocked in waters that may not fit the ideal—if there's good food and cover for them.

In water where more than one of these species lives, and ideal temperature ranges coincide, you can expect to catch *any* of these fish on flies that imitate their common natural foods.

Here are the temperature ranges the chief warm-water fish prefer.

> smallmouth bass—60°–70°
> largemouth bass—65°–75°
> Kentucky spotted bass—60°–75°
> rock bass—60°–70°
> bluegill—65°–75°
> crappie—60°–75°
> northern pike—50°–70°
> chain pickerel—60°–80°
> muskie—60°–70°
> walleye pike—60°–70°
> yellow perch—60°–70°
> white bass—58°–68°
> striped bass—55°–70°
> common sunfish—65°–75°

Bass are amazingly adaptable to various water types and sizes. Other than in the obvious large lakes and streams, you can expect to find them in such a variety of places as farm ponds, ditches, canals, golf-course water hazards, irrigation ponds and canals, brackish lagoons, duck ponds, swamps, oxbows, livestock water ponds, spring creeks, condo ponds, park ponds, sloughs, flooded quarry pits, flooded agricultural chops, flooded strip pits, below dams, and a host of other places. That's why I said you'll most likely live near some decent bass water wherever you live.

Each type of water is unique and offers its own rewards to the adventurous bass fisherman; and each has its own personality, its own "look," its special food chain.

A pair of spawning largemouth bass. The male is smaller; the female selects a typical spawning site.

Such untypical waters are often underfished; they'll sometimes have more fish, fish more willing to strike your offerings, and even *huge* surprises. Also, because such bass see mostly other baits, lures, and methods, they don't hesitate to strike flies.

Bass usually mature at two or three years. Males are somewhat smaller than females of the same age, especially those that are four years and older. Mature largemouth males average about 1½ pounds and only occasionally reach or exceed three pounds. The female largemouth may average three pounds and often exceeds five or six pounds in both its northern and southern ranges. Smallmouth usually run about half to two-thirds the size of those largemouth averages.

Bass normally spawn once a year after maturity, usually in late winter (February/March) in the South and late spring (June/July) in their northern homes. This is a function of rising water temperatures. When the winter warming water reaches 60° to the mid-70°s in the shallow areas (one to six feet) preferred by bass, spawning occurs.

The male selects a nest site along a sheltered shoreline and with his tail digs a shallow depression in the sand or fine gravel. He then invites the female to it. About twenty-four hours after spawning occurs, the female drifts away; then the male guards the nest from egg-stealing predators and "fans" the eggs to keep them well-oxygenated and free of silt.

After the fry hatch the male continues to protect them for a few days, then leaves the area. On occasion, he may attack and even eat some of his own fry but I believe that this is his method of making them more wary and scattering the school into small groups, which are less vulnerable to predators.

Just prior to the spawning period, during it, and shortly afterward, bass are active, aggressive, and in more or less shallow water. This is probably the most popular time to catch more and larger bass on flies. Fly fishing a bass bed brings an almost sure strike from the more protective male or the less protective female.

Thereafter, though, spawning stress causes both sexes to go into a post-natal depression and period of exhaustion. They swim to deeper water. Some females even die during this period. The survivors rest or refrain from much if any feeding for two to six weeks. When this period passes they gradually return to feed normally until the next spawning season the following year.

The best fly fishing depends when bass find ideal water temperatures with a good supply of food and oxygen. If the water they find comfortable is deep (fifteen to fifty feet, or even deeper), then fly fishing for them can be difficult or impossible. But if the shallow water (one to fifteen feet) stays in a comfortable temperature range, fly fishing will be excellent.

Streams and lakes that have stable water levels, are not very large, or do not have a deep average depth are certainly the best places to fly fish for bass. These waters are usually filled with plenty of food, good aquatic life, a varied and productive shoreline, and lots of shallow-water structure. These features allow bass to do their day-to-day resting and eating in safety and convenience. Bass are also easier to locate and fish to with flies in these compact, cover-rich waters. Larger and deeper waters, especially manmade reservoirs, may have more and larger bass but in these places the fish can be difficult to locate and reach with flies because the water is so deep and there is so little cover. Except during a brief period just before spawning, during spawning, and in late fall, bass in these large, deep lakes prefer to live suspended over deep-water structures. Such big-water lakes may have many miles of nearly fishless shoreline for most of the year. Even when you can locate bass over deep structure, they are not as easily and pleasurably caught with a fly rod. Start with one to fifty-acre lakes or small streams; work your way gradually into the large ones as your skills, knowledge, and experience increase.

Bass are magnificently designed to detect and eat aquatic and terrestrial foods. They are live-animal eaters and seldom if ever eat dead animal matter or plants. They have a neatly split pallet, feeding most regularly on other fish, crayfish, and insects but nearly always willing to spice up their daily meal with many other foods. Bass will eat mice, snakes, crabs, worms, leeches, eels, lamphreys, salamanders, birds, lizards, grasshoppers, bats, turtles, frogs, baby alligators, and even each other!

It is their interest in this amazing variety of sizes, shapes, colors, and actions of live foods that makes bass so popular with artificial-lure and fly fishermen. Bass will at least once strike almost any fly you cast to them.

And along with their feeding preferences, bass also have another side—a curious personality and bad temper that says, "Stay out of my yard," that is un-neighborly toward predators. A clever and patient user of artificial lures or flies who understands this other side of its personality can make a bass attack a lure even if the fish is stuffed with fresh food. This aggressive character trait adds an exciting, extra dimension to our pleasure in fly fishing for bass.

No other fish has a more perfect body and mouth for ambushing live food on top of, in, or along the bottom of water. Bass won't go long distances with great speed; but they are blindingly quick and have unbelievable maneuverability. They locate their prey primarily by extra-keen senses of sight and sound. Most experts agree that sight is their most important sense but in most bass habitats, lack of light, murky water quality, a preponderance of vegetation and other underwater structures keep them from seeing their prey at any distance—usually more than two or three feet. Observing bass carefully for many years, I have come to believe that most *hear* their food first; then they set their ambush or swim to intercept their prey.

Bass hear high-frequency sounds (noise) with an inner ear similar to yours and low-frequency sounds (water-pressure changes) with a series of lateral-line nerve sensors.

Exterior anatomy of a bass.

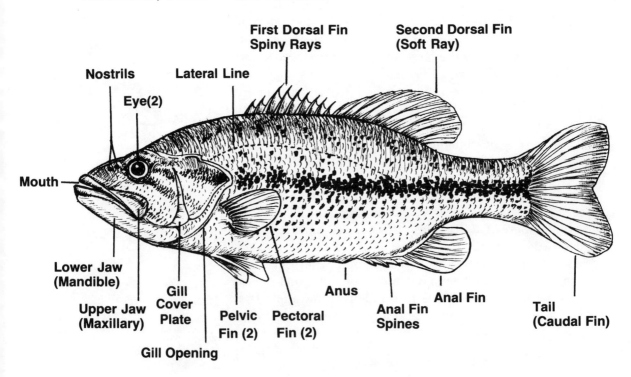

First Dorsal Fin
Spiny Rays

Second Dorsal Fin
(Soft Ray)

Nostrils

Lateral Line

Eye(2)

Mouth

Lower Jaw
(Mandible)

Upper Jaw
(Maxillary)

Gill
Cover
Plate

Pelvic
Fin (2)

Pectoral
Fin (2)

Anus

Anal Fin
Spines

Anal Fin

Tail
(Caudal Fin)

Gill Opening

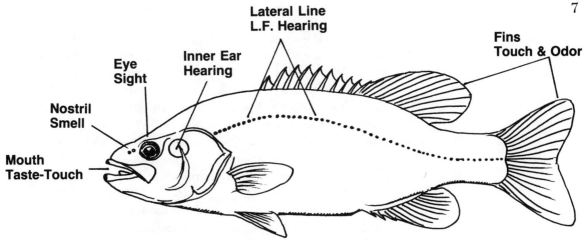

A bass's senses.

This hearing-sensor system allows a bass to become alerted to the presence of prey, locate its position, determine its size, shape, and even the number of such objects before it ever sees the prey. As a fly lands on the water, a bass from one to twenty feet away will hear the impact with its inner ear. If the fly begins to move across the surface making sounds that you can hear, that bass surely hears the sounds even quicker and more clearly (since water transmits sound better than air).

Bass will sense, hear, or feel the movements of an underwater fly with their lateral-line sensors. Larger or bulkier flies and faster movement of them are easiest for a bass to detect with this sensor system. If the fly strikes such underwater obstacles as rocks, weeds, tree limbs, and stumps, the impact noise will be heard by the bass's inner ear. Flies equipped with revolving spinner blades or a wiggle-bill design are effective low-frequency generators.

Bass can quickly and easily find and catch good sound-generating flies in dark or turbid waters. Never let the lack of water clarity or night discourage you from fly fishing an area you know bass inhabit. Generally, bass are easier to fool in waters where their vision is restricted. With the right flies and method you can catch bass in water so "muddy" you can almost walk on it, or when it is so dark you cannot see your hand in front of your face. Just give the bass a good chance to hear your fly. Use a "noisy" fly and a highly visible fly, and retrieve at a speed that will give them time to react. You'll catch bass.

A bass's two eyes give it both good binocular vision to the front and monocular vision plus peripheral vision to its sides. Bass see colors very well, especially highly visible dark or bright colors. Colors or combinations of colors that always seem effective on artificial lures and flies are black, white, yellow, red, chartreuse, purple, and blue. Light-reflective materials such as spinner blades, mylar strips, and spoons are effective sight exciters; these mirror-metallic or reflective surfaces simulate life and action, which bass associate with struggling or escaping foods such as crippled minnows or panic-stricken fish.

Bass can see their prey and predators very well—as well as conditions permit. But remember this: they can see no farther through the water than you can. If you are looking down and through the water or underneath the surface with a face mask and can only see one foot clearly, that's also all a bass sees. It's their combined sense of hearing with sight that makes you think they see better than you can in water.

Bass normally prefer low levels of sunlight to open sunlight. At midday they seek out shade or go deeper, where light does not penetrate well. In very clear water they often resort to night feeding to avoid various dangers.

Sometimes you'll see a bass leap from the water to intercept a fly in clear water. Their jumping and vaulting ability enables them to catch flying insects, birds, or other creatures in the air. If you fly fish when they're behaving this way, you'll have bass leap up and catch your fly above the water or strike the instant it lands on the surface. This makes for extremely exciting fly fishing!

Once your fly is on or under the clear water, its color, size, and movement become the key factors for inducing bass to strike.

Since bass see farther above and below in clear and well-lighted water, in such conditions they can detect both your presence and any fraud in your line, leader, or fly. Be aware then that sight and sound can work for or against you. Try to stay out of sight and quiet while you present your fly to the bass. Noises you make walking on banks or wading or by paddling or rowing, or by banging parts of the boat, and noises from an electric motor or gas engine, all alert bass. Most times they're frightened by such noise, though occasionally some of these sounds will attract them. Being quiet is usually the best approach to *any* fishing.

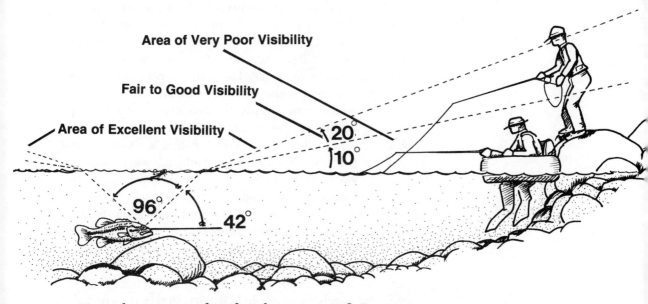

How else are sound and sight important? Bass are designed to detect food and danger in the water; above the water is a more or less foreign zone, just as water is foreign to land and air creatures. So bass are more apprehensive or afraid of objects over the water, especially moving and brightly reflective objects. You're more likely to frighten a bass by allowing it to see you or your fly line in the air above them than you will be wading too close to them. You will often see bass bolt and dash to cover at the sight of your fly line as you false cast—yet they will smash the fly that plops loudly and visible over them in the water.

Bass also use their senses of smell, taste, and touch to identify food or foe. They have an excellent sense of smell and use it as a third test when they inspect your fly—particularly when sight is inhibited. Bass usually smell more when they cannot see well; they become very selective and cautious when fishing pressure on them is hard, and they will use smell more at such times, too.

Flies that have unnatural odors will be less effective than those that smell like the environment or like natural foods if bass are using their sense of smell for any reason.

It is currently popular among baitcasters and spin-fishermen to use scented plastic lures or to spray their artificial lures with chemical formulas of fish-attracting scents. Many bass fishermen claim this improves their

How bass see above the surface in various light-ray refractions.
At 10° off horizontal, very poor—especially on dark or windy days.
At 20° off horizontal, fair if the light is good and the surface calm.
At over 20°, they see very well.

catch. Fly fishers are usually more conservative about this practice yet it is important to know that bass do under certain circumstances hit or refuse flies because of their odors. Because most flies are made of soft, water-absorbent feathers, hair, and synthetics, adding these scents may make them a gummy, smelly, lifeless mass. I advise you simply to deodorize your flies by rubbing on local algae, mud, moss, or sand to mask the odor of a new fly. After you've fished a fly for a few minutes it has usually cleansed itself, anyway; and once one or two fish are hooked, I'm sure most all of the unnatural odor is removed.

A bass has an amazing sensitivity to touch on its body and mouth, much greater than that of a trout or char. This means: use flies that have soft, realistic textures. Weighted lures—like plastic worms, rubber worms, pork rinds, soft rubber plugs—are consistently excellent bass catchers when fished very slowly or when the bass's underwater strike is not sight- but feel-detected by the fisherman.

Since most bass flies are soft and chewy because of the tying material used, they make excellent bass catchers. A bass bug made of clipped deer hair will nearly always be held in a bass's mouth *two or three times* longer than a hard plastic or wooden fly or lure of the same size and shape. In fact, bass can inhale and exhale a hard fly or lure so fast it's easy to think they actually missed it. I've often observed this faster-than-a-blink reaction when testing new fly designs on bass I keep in large aquariums and ponds.

There are times when bass become so frenzied or aggressive they will ignore texture but the fly fisher should never gamble on hard over soft flies.

One more thought about the bass's senses. Sense responses to artificial lures and flies vary as water temperatures go much below or above the ideal, especially the colder extreme. Bass become slower, so you should place your fly, move it, and respond to the strike with slower timing. In *very* cold water, place your fly closer to the bass, and move it much more slowly and less erratically. Give the bass more time to take the fly into its mouth before you strike. Think of how your hands work when they're warm or very cold when you tie a knot: in the cold, they're numb, cold, and less efficient. Bass are that way, too.

A basic but solid understanding of bass will help you to approach fly fishing for them with more confidence. Fly fishing will let you imitate the enormous variety of live foods on which the bass feeds; if bass eat half-inch-long insects or eight-inch-long minnows, the fly fisher can match these—and anything in between. I hope you'll find, as I have, that fly fishing is actually the *most versatile* method available for fishing artificial lures for bass.

Successful fly fishing for bass, then, will result when you understand the life patterns and rhythms of this fish and then use fly tackle and flies in a manner they cannot resist. If you do so, you will be rewarded with one of the most consistently enjoyable ways to catch our most popular freshwater gamefish . . . as well as the dozen or so associated species.

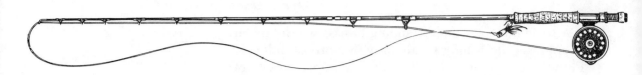

2
Fly Fishing and Fly Tackle

You must understand the principles of fly fishing for bass and outfit yourself properly or you'll face a lot of frustration, especially if you're a beginner or spin or baitcasting bass fisherman. Even as a capable fly fisher, I struggled for many years because I didn't know how the fly-tackle casting system for bass worked.

Most artificial lures are cast by the fisherman and land where he thinks a fish may be waiting to strike his offering. This cast is usually thirty to one hundred feet. We cannot throw a feather that far because it is too light and air-resistant, but we can throw a stone the size of a golf ball that distance easily. If you fix the stone to the feather, you can propel the feather that distance. This is what happens when a fisherman casts an artificial lure or fly to the target area.

There are two kinds of casting. Each method uses a rod, reel, line, and lure but beyond these common factors they differ drastically. Baitcasting, spin-casting, and spinning use an artificial lure that has some weight. When cast, the lure pulls the attached line (which is more or less weightless) off the fishing reel. Then, using his rod and reel, the fisherman animates the weighted lure to swim toward him.

Fly fishing works on an opposite principle. The "fly," which is a simple term for an artificial that may imitate all sorts of foods, not just flies, is made out of feathers and/or hair; so it has virtually no weight. In fly fishing, it is the fly line that has the weight needed for casting; the line (like the stone) with weightless fly attached, is cast to the target. The fly line pulls the fly with it to that spot.

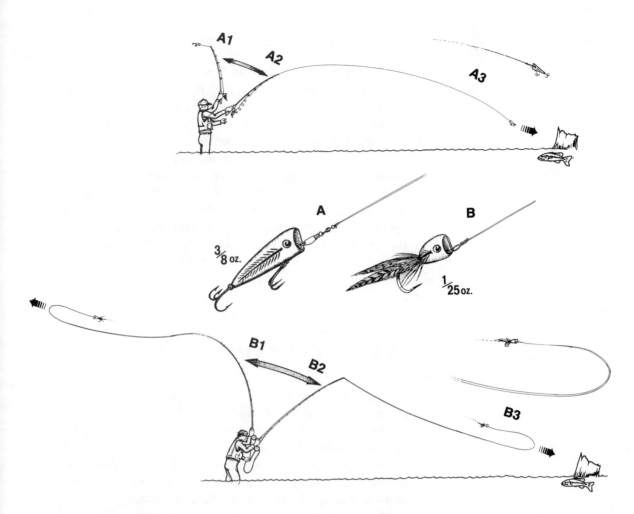

In fly fishing, the line pulls the fly; in lure casting, the lure pulls the line. This distinction is basic and important.

There is another central difference. You begin to cast a lure with your rod tip; when you cast, the lure pulls the line it needs off the reel. Then, turning the handle of the reel, the fisherman begins to animate and retrieve the lure by winding line back onto the reel. This retrieve moves the lure through the water back to the tip of the rod.

To cast a fly, you must extend some line from the tip of your fly rod and considerably more must be loose between the reel and the first guide. The fly line is cast with the long fly rod up and behind the fisherman and then cast down and forward to the target. The weight of the line from the tip of the rod to the fly pulls out the loose line between the reel and the first guide. Then the fly is animated and retrieved by hand pulls on the fly line, *not* by reeling in the line.

Casting Lures and Flies

A is the spinning-lure caster; B is the fly caster. Caster A1 begins his cast with a weighted lure at the tip of his spinning rod. Caster A2 strokes his rod toward the target, from A1 to A2, to direct his weighted lure properly. When the caster releases his hold on the weightless line, the lure pulls it from A2 to the target area, A3.

The fly caster, B1, with his extended length of fly line (B2 to B1) strokes the weighted fly line and weightless fly up and back; he pauses until the line straightens, then strokes B1 to B2 toward the target. The rod stops at B2 but the line unrolls, pulling the weightless fly toward the target, B3.

Neither during the cast nor during the retrieve is the fly reel used. And the fly line is not pulled its entire length back to your rod, as it is in baitcasting.

Though fly fishing is clearly a more manual method of casting, and requires more practice to master, it has a host of advantages. There is no limit to what can be imitated, from a gnat to a ten-inch-long shiner. Since bass eat such a wide variety of live foods, this range of possible imitations is extremely significant. Also, because flies are typically made of soft lifelike materials, the greatest realism is possible. Finally, the long, sensitive rod and hands-on method is just more challenging and fun.

FLY-TACKLE COMPONENTS

A fly-tackle system will consist of the fly, the fly line, the fly reel, and the fly rod.

The Fly. All flies are relatively weightless and, depending upon what they imitate, vary in size, shape, density, color, texture, and design. Most bass flies use a single hook, though a few styles call for double or tandem-double hooks for more efficient hooking.

There are two main categories of flies: those that float, sometimes called "dry" flies, and those that sink, called "wet" flies. Fly fishers for bass should keep these six groups in mind.

Dry fly. Rests mostly above and on the surface.

Surface fly. Floats at the surface but mostly just under it.

Floating diver. Floats at the surface but when retrieved it dives to some depth.

Swimming fly. Sinks below the surface at various rates of retrieve and, when pulled, it has a swimming action.

Bottom fly. Sinks rapidly so as to reach the bottom quickly. It is retrieved or "crawled" back along the bottom.

Jig fly. This fly has a special heavy head that sinks the fly rapidly. When retrieved with a pull/pause/pull motion in mid-water or near the bottom it has an up-and-down swimming or bottom-hopping motion.

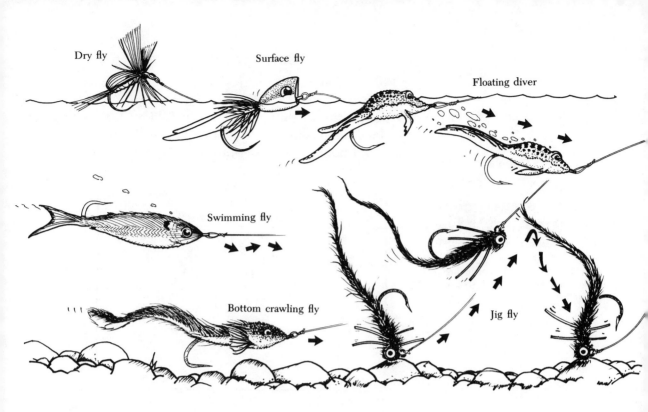

Dry fly

Surface fly

Floating diver

Swimming fly

Bottom crawling fly

Jig fly

Since flies vary in hook size, wind resistance, weight, and length, they will affect the weight and design of fly line that must be used. The fly line must be significantly heavier than the combined weight of the fly and the air resistance it creates if the casting process is to work. Heavier fly lines are required to cast larger flies.

FLY-LINE COMPONENTS

The three components of a fly-line system are the line, the backing, and the leader.

The fly line is the key component in any fly-fishing tackle system because the fly line controls the fly. Lines are easy to understand and, when you do, you'll never regret the effort taken to learn them when the rewards of fly fishing begin.

All fly lines are designed in particular lengths, weights, densities, shapes, strengths, and colors to do specific jobs.

Fly-line Sizes (Weights). Fly lines are manufactured in fifteen standardized sizes or weights, which are designated 1, 2, 3, on up to 15. The larger numbers weigh more. This numerical code refers to what the first thirty feet of any fly line weighs.

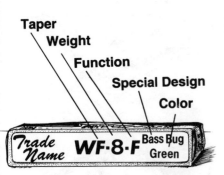

Taper
Weight
Function
Special Design
Color

Trade Name WF·8·F Bass Bug Green

AFTMA Fly Line Code—including taper, weight, function, and special design or color.

Fly-line weight is a relative guide to the performance of the line, not its pound-test strength. Remember: the fly line *is* the casting weight in fly fishing. Generally speaking, larger line sizes will cast larger flies best, farther, and better in winds—just as heavier lures can be cast farther than lighter ones.

AFTMA FLY LINE STANDARDS		
#	Wt.	Range
1	60	54-66
2	80	74-86
3	100	94-106
4	120	114-126
5	140	134-146
6	160	152-168
7	185	177-193
8	210	202-218
9	240	230-250
10	280	270-290
11	330	318-342
12	380	368-392

Weight in grains — based on first 30 feet (exclusive of any level tip). Range allows for acceptable manufacturing tolerances.

Fly-line Construction. The modern fly line has a flexible level *core* of braided nylon or similar material that provides the strength and length needed. The core is usually twenty to forty-pound test and eighty to 120 feet long. These vary in size and purpose for each type of fly line. To the core is molded a plastic—usually soft, tough vinyl—that provides the *coating*. The coating gives the fly line most of its casting weight, its shape, color, size, flexibility, and density; it also reduces friction on rod guides, air, and water. This coating makes the fly line thick when compared to other fishing lines; but this, rather than being a handicap, provides the fly fisher with various handling and control advantages.

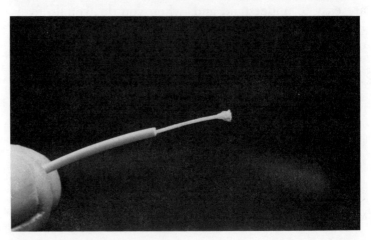

Fly-line Shapes. All modern fly lines have a level core and a molded coating that may or may not vary in shape and thickness. This coating variation or shape has three basic designs: level, double taper, and weight forward. These designs affect the presentation and distance potential of all lines.

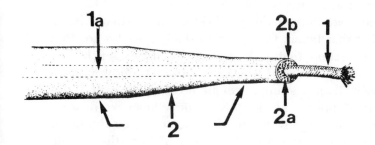

Parts of a Fly Line

1. Braided core
1A. The core is level and gives the line its strength.
2. Coating provides most of the fly-line's weight and shape
2A. Coating composition determines density.
2B. Coating finish reduces friction in the guides and on the water

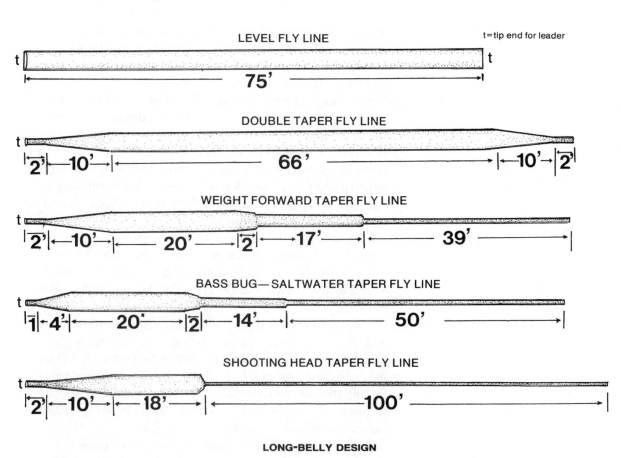

LEVEL FLY LINE

t=tip end for leader

t — 75' — t

DOUBLE TAPER FLY LINE

t — 2' — 10' — 66' — 10' — 2'

WEIGHT FORWARD TAPER FLY LINE

t — 2' — 10' — 20' — 2' — 17' — 39'

BASS BUG— SALTWATER TAPER FLY LINE

t — 1 — 4' — 20' — 2 — 14' — 50'

SHOOTING HEAD TAPER FLY LINE

t — 2' — 10' — 18' — 100'

LONG-BELLY DESIGN

Typical fly-line options.

The *level fly line* (L) is just that—consistent coating over the core in its entire length. Level lines cast with a heavy-handed feel and fall on the water with a hard or jerky movement because the tip section is as heavy as the belly of the fly line. This line is used mainly for bait fishing, panfishing, trolling, and limited bass bugging. Its main attribute is low cost.

The *double-taper* design (DT) has a level core but a coating that tapers from thin to thick at each end, to a center section that is largest and remains level. The taper allows the fly to be cast with considerably more delicacy than a similar weight level fly line. It is tapered at both ends for economic efficiency. Reason: since most of the wear on a fly line occurs on the finish and coating of the first thirty feet of line, the double taper can be reversed on the fly reel and you get two lines for the price of one. The double taper can be used for bass fly fishing but I don't particularly recommend it for this; it does not cast larger bass flies with the ease and efficiency of another design.

The *weight-forward taper* (WF) has a level core but a coating design that makes it more functional than either the level line or double taper. It has a tapered tip section similar to one end of the double taper; then it has a large-diameter level "belly" of some thirty to fifty feet, which tapers back to a small-diameter level-running or shooting portion for another fifty feet. (Study the diagram if this sounds confusing.)

This design allows good fly presentation like a double taper but, because of the thin diameter past the "casting weight" belly, allows more casting distance as well. The thin line reduces friction in the fly-rod guides. For most short and medium-length casting and roll casting, the weight forward does everything that a double taper will do. It provides good casting and roll-casting dynamics and delicate presentations of fly to water. When more distance is needed, the belly is given an extra casting thrust and its faster-moving weight pulls the thinner section—which is usually held in coils in the caster's hand—out through the rod guides to the required distance. Weight-forward lines were once called the "power-casting lines" and considered not as good for delicacy or roll casting as the double taper; this is not true for weight forwards made today.

The standard weight forward, since it has a similar thin tip taper to that of the double taper, will cast bass flies well but is not ideal for the larger flies.

The more versatile and modern weight-forward line has three important variations. They are the bug or salt-water taper, the long-belly taper, and the shooting-head taper.

The *bug or saltwater taper* is a weight-forward line especially designed to cast and present heavier and more wind-resistant flies, especially the typical bass bug. It is also designed to cast efficiently from twenty to seventy feet without false casting (making one or more air casts to extend extra line past the rod tip). The bug taper has a shorter and coarser tip taper than the same weight DT or WF. The belly portion is shorter, heavier, and a bit larger in diameter. The running or shooting section is quite small for fast, long, line shoots. This puts more forceful line weight closer to the fly for better casting and presentation of the large bass flies. This coarse-tip design can cause the fly to strike the water a bit harder but most bass are not frightened by noisy presentation.

Long-belly weight-forward (LB) lines are one of the most recent innovations in fly-line design. As the name implies, this line has a longer belly than either standard or bug-taper weight forwards. This is specifically for better rod-loading balance for longer casts. It was conceived to complement the higher performance capabilities of today's graphite and boron-fiber fly rods. When seventy to 100-feet casts are needed to reach a fish, this fly line is better than either the standard or bug weight forward.

Weight-forward shooting head (SH) lines are primarily for casting and shooting fly lines extra-long distances quickly and without false-casting. Such lines consist of twenty to forty feet (thirty feet is average) of fly line spliced or tied to 100 feet of a special, extra-thin level line called "shooting line" or twenty to forty-pound-test shooting monofilament.

Such fly lines have two particular uses in bass fly fishing: for casting extra-fast-sinking lines safely and conveniently; and when bass fly fishers need to make thirty to eighty-feet open-water retrieves.

All these fly-line shapes are useful to fly fishers for bass. However, for most purposes the bug weight-forward taper is the best first choice because it is specifically designed for most bass fly-fishing situations. The level does a fair job of hammering bass flies into the wind and at close ranges. Double and standard weight-forward and long-belly weight-forward each will cast bass flies if the flies are not too heavy, large, or wind-resistant. Another option: if you can't find a bug taper, cut about half the taper off the tip (four to eight feet) of a regular weight forward and you'll have a reasonably good substitute.

FLY-LINE FUNCTION

Fly lines also help to control the fly's position in the water column. Fly lines, as well as flies, float or sink. There are three general types—floating, neutral or very-slow-sinking fly
lines, and fast-sinking fly lines. There is also a sinking-tip float-belly fly line.

Floating Fly Line (F). This line will float at the water surface. It is primarily used to fish floating flies but may also be used for diving and sinking flies if they only need to be fished in shallow water. This is a useful and popular fly line for bass fly fishing.

Intermediate (I). This neutral-density fly line weighs about the same as water. When its coating is dressed with a fly-line flotant, this line will float low in the sur-face film and be virtually the same as a floating line. When not dressed, it will sink slowly and allow you to control a sinking fly's swim angle. This is not a popular line for general bass fly fishing.

Sinking-Tip Line (F/S). The tip section of this line sinks and the belly portion floats. The floating belly portion makes this line easier to use than a full-sinking line when you do not have to get the fly very deep. The sinking tip may be from five to fifteen feet long, with different lengths designed to make the fly sink to a par-ticular depth. Sinking-tip lines are manufactured in sev-eral tip-density choices (sink rates) for slow, medium, fast-sinking, and extra-fast-sinking. This range varies from about two to eight inches deep a second. This *versatile and important bass fly-fishing line design* will enable you to fish floating and floating-diving flies uniquely as well as all other sinking types.

Sinking Fly Line (S). The sinking line is primarily de-signed to pull or sink the fly down to deep water and hold it there while the fly is fished. Sinking lines are available in various sink rates from two to three inches per second to eight to ten inches per second. Many wet flies do not sink quickly; but modern sinking lines have

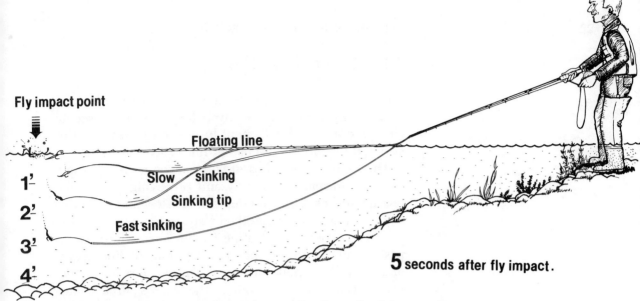

Fly impact point

Floating line

Slow sinking

Sinking tip

Fast sinking

1'
2'
3'
4'

5 seconds after fly impact.

opened up a large new area of water depth to fly fishers. Sinking lines are important where bass frequently move to deep and open-water areas of both lakes and large rivers.

If you cast level (L), double-taper (DT), or weight-forward fly lines in the three basic densities—floating, slow-sinking, and fast-sinking of the same weight—you will see big differences. This is because each has a different density due to the size and content of the coating. The floating line is larger in diameter and more buoyant because its plastic coating contains microscopic glass air bubbles. It will feel larger in diameter and lighter as you cast it than the others. The slow-sinking line will be smaller in diameter and its coating will be 100-percent plastic or have a few microscopic particles of metal—usually lead powder—mixed in it. The fast-sinking line will be even smaller diameter, having less plastic and more metal powder in it to increase its density for faster sink rates. The sinking lines will feel heavier when you cast them but each is the same weight per foot as the floaters.

The floating line is the most enjoyable to cast and fish (it's easier to lift off the surface of the water than a sinking line under the surface); as line densities increase above, say, #7 and #8, the lines become more troublesome to manage well. The floating line glides more smoothly through the air but will not cast as far for the same weight as the sinking fly line because it has more resistance on rod guides and through the air. This is because of its larger diameter.

Densities of Four Fly-Line Types
1. Floating
2. Intermediate—slow sinking
3. Sinking tip
4. Sinking

FLY-LINE COLOR

The large, highly visible fly lines must puzzle the prospective fly fisher, especially if he has grown used to clear gossamer monofilament lure-casting lines. Yet this size and visibility will enable him to fly fish better.

The fly line works best if you can see it clearly when casting, presenting your fly and retrieving it, and detecting strikes. Its diameter size and coating color are keys to much of this method's success.

Popular colors for floating fly lines are white, ivory, pastel, yellow, green, peach, grey, tan, or fluorescent orange, yellow, pink, or green. These colors are particularly visible in the air and on the water's surface. Bass are not usually alarmed by them. When viewed from underwater, objects floating on the surface in daylight appear more or less as grey or dark shadow lines; to demonstrate this, hold a bright-colored line between you and a light source.

Some floating fly lines are available in dark green or dark brown. These are hard to see but may be necessary for spooky fish in bright sunlight, extra-clear water, and calm surfaces. You can also change light-colored lines to darker ones simply by applying such fabric dyes as Rit or Putnam. As you master special casts, keeping the fly line from alarming the bass becomes relatively easy.

Sink-tip and full-sinking fly lines are usually made of more natural, less contrasting colors because lines at bass eye level are generally more visible to fish. Since most or all of the sinking line is underwater, bright colors are not nearly as useful as they are for the floating line.

LEADERS

The leader provides a low-visibility link between the heavy visible line tip and the fly. It has five functions:

To assist the fly line in casting and proper presentation of the fly;

To provide a link of low-visibility line on or in the water between the thick fly line's tip and the fly;

To assist in floating and/or sinking the fly;

To provide the strongest flexible connection between

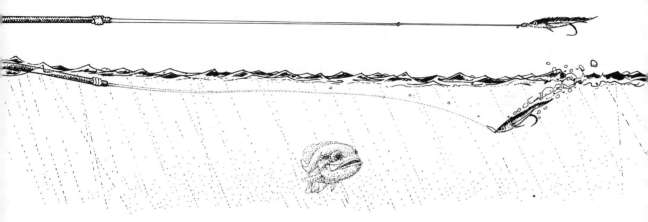

fly line and the fly. This flexibility allows the fly to act most like a living food; and

To provide a smaller-diameter line section that will pass through the fly hook's eye for convenience in tying on the fly.

Modern leaders are made of nylon monofilament or braided nylon monofilaments. There are two general shapes, level and tapered. The level leader, like the level fly line, is simple and low cost but has limits. Tapered leaders are the most popular and functional for bass and most other types of fly fishing. Tapered leaders are made three ways:

Knotted—sections of monofilament nylon, level but in varying diameters, are tied together to effect a taper shape;

Knotless taper—single strand of nylon monofilament is tapered by extrusion, grinding, or acid etching;

Braided taper—multiple level or tapered strands of monofilament are braided or twisted to form the leader butt and midsection.

Three types of tapered leaders

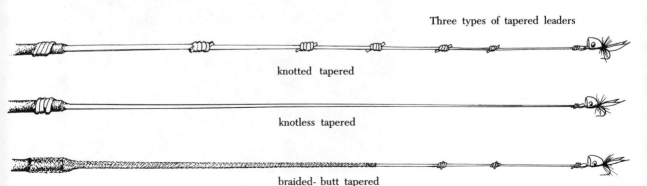

knotted tapered

knotless tapered

braided- butt tapered

A tapered leader has three general parts—the butt, body or midsection, and the tip. The tip section may or may not have another part called the tippet.

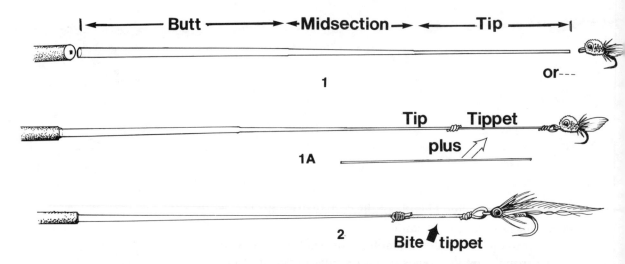

1. Leader parts
1A. With tippet
2. Leader with bite tippet

The *butt section* has the largest diameter. This is for matching and connecting the fly-line's tip and providing a smooth continuous transfer of casting energy from fly line to fly.

The *midsection* or *body area* has the greatest taper— for the deceleration of fly and graduation to tip.

The *tip* (end section of a leader) is the most flexible and smallest-diameter portion of the leader; it allows the most natural action and provides the best sight deception of the fly.

The *tippet* is a level length of nylon monofilament similar or smaller than the tip of the leader. It is tied to the end of the leader.

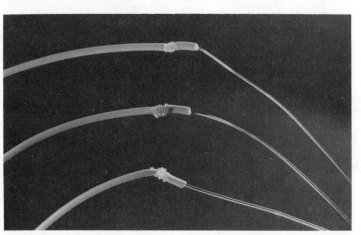

Leader butt to fly-line flexibility.

Leader butt is too flexible.

Leader butt and fly-line flexibility match.

Leader butt is too stiff.

LEADER TIPPET AND FLY SIZE
(For optimum casting, presentation, and fishing performance)

Leader Tip or Tippet	X Code	Pound Test	Fly-Hook Sizes
(Diameter in thousandths of an inch) /9.9x9			
.003	8X	1.2	24,26,28,32
.004	7X	2	20,22,24,26
.005	6X	3	16,18,20,22
.006	5X	4	14,16,18
.007	4X	6	12,14,16
.008	3X	8	10,12,14
.009	2X	10	6,8,10
.010	1X	12	2,4,6
.011	0X	13	1/0,2,4
.012	X1	15	2/0,1/0,2
.013	X2	16	3/0,2/0,1/0,2
.014	X3	18	5/0,4/0,3/0,2/0
.015	X4	20	6/0,5/0,4/0,3/0

(Practical bass sizes: .008 through .015)

Based on monofilament nylon, Umpqua, and L.L. Bean product

Note: This chart is a simple guideline. Fly-hook wire sizes, hook-shank lengths, extra weighting, and material designs, as well as variations in leader-material stiffness, all affect performance. In situations where water is very clear and calm and fish are very selective, longer, smaller-diameter leaders and tippets are more effective because they are less visible and allow the fly to look and act more natural. In heavy cover areas, leader abrasion is a problem. Use the largest diameter tip or tippet that is practical.

BASS FLY-LINE AND LEADER CHART

Type of Fly Line	Leader Length (Feet)	Place to Use
Floating Bass and Salt Water (WF)	7½ to 9	Most bass, pike, and panfish streams ponds, lakes, and saltwater areas
Sinking Tip (DT, WF)	4 to 6	To fish most waters listed above from 3 to 10 feet deep
Full Sinking (DT, WF, ST)	2 to 6	To fish most waters listed above, 4 to 20 feet deep

Tie on a tippet for the following reasons:

To make the leader tip longer for softer presentation and better deception—and to help absorb the shock of the strike; think of it as a variable performance tuning section.

To make the end of your leader smaller for better deception, and provide freer movement of the fly in the water;

To restore the original tip length when it has been shortened by fly knots, wind knots or breakage;

To create dropper lengths for tying two or more flies on the leader's tip section; and

To extend the life of your leader; it is easier and less expensive to tie on a tippet section than to buy and tie new leaders when a tip is used up or damaged.

A *bite tippet* is a heavier or tougher section of nylon or wire tied to the leader's end or tip. This will prevent certain fish that may inhabit bass water from cutting the fly off with sharp teeth, scales, head plates, or fins. These species include northern pike, muskie, pickerel, bowfin, gar, tarpon, and snook. Also, rough rock and barnacles fray and cut leaders in some waters. A bite tippet is usually made of nylon monofilament, thirty to 100-pound test, or plastic-coated braided or solid wire, ten to thirty-pound strength, in lengths of six to twelve inches, or more as needed.

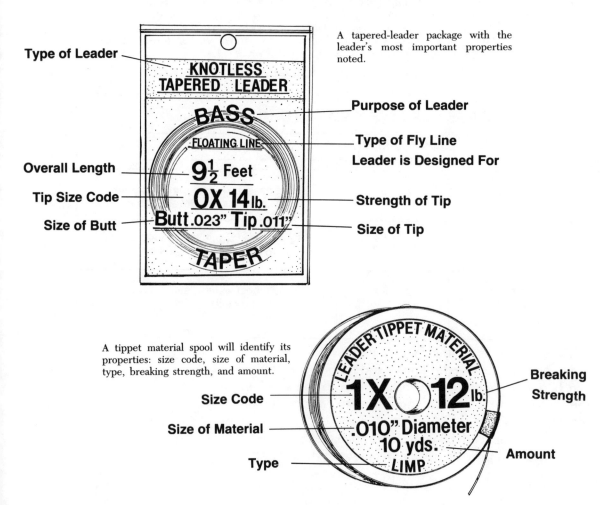

Type of Leader

A tapered-leader package with the leader's most important properties noted.

KNOTLESS TAPERED LEADER

BASS

Purpose of Leader

FLOATING LINE

Type of Fly Line Leader is Designed For

9½ Feet

Overall Length

0X 14 lb.

Tip Size Code

Strength of Tip

Butt .023" Tip .011"

Size of Butt

Size of Tip

TAPER

A tippet material spool will identify its properties: size code, size of material, type, breaking strength, and amount.

LEADER TIPPET MATERIAL

Size Code

1X 12 lb.

Breaking Strength

Size of Material

.010" Diameter 10 yds.

Type

LIMP

Amount

In addition to the leader that is tied to the fly line's tip, you should also have extra leader or tippet material with you for modifications. This tippet material is sold in convenient spools varying in diameter and strength usually from .003″ to .016,″ which approximately covers two, four, six, eight, ten, twelve, fourteen, sixteen, eighteen, and twenty-pound test. This extra material is also coded with X + a number—that is, 3X, 5X, and so forth. This simple code relates to the diameter of the material. Fishermen are often concerned most with the diameter of the leader so this X code is especially valuable to them. Nearly every year the ratio of pound test to diameter in these products is improving.

Floating Fly-line Leaders. The bass or heavy-butt knotless tapered leader is the most functional choice for floating-fly-line fishing. It has been specifically designed like the bug weight-forward floating fly line to cast and fish bass flies properly. The properties of this leader are:

The butt end is similar to the tip of the fly line in flexibility and diameter;

The butt section is long and heavy; this helps transfer energy from fly line to fly on the back or forward cast;

No knots to tangle during casting or to hang on water objects or to fail during the fight. Leader knots will catch on weed or other objects in typical bass water;

Made of the most durable abrasion-resistant monofilament available;

Tip has highest knot strength and high ratio of pound test for diameter;

Its color should blend well with the color of the water. A watery olive green is best;

Length should be seven to ten feet. The shorter length is best when only a short cast is needed, when the fish cannot see well, in windy weather, and to cast better and present wind-resistant bass flies. The longer lengths are better in clear, calm, unobstructed areas, and with smaller, less wind-resistant flies.

Bass leaders much longer than your fly rod may require that the butt section be pulled inside the tip guides when you land a bass. Should the bass dash away or jump at that critical point, the fly-line-to-leader knot may catch on your guide, causing you to lose the fish, the fly, and perhaps damage your rod tip. It's best to keep your leader the length of your fly rod or shorter. Note: When purchasing a leader it is well to know that it will be shortened six to twelve inches by the knots used to tie it to the line and the fly—so allow for this loss.

The best sink-tip or sinking-line tapered leader for casting and fishing most bass flies effectively is a six-foot knotless taper with a short butt and midsection and a long tip section. Such a leader design gives a good fly line-to-leader energy transfer and allows the sinking fly line to pull the leader underwater with reasonable ease. The leader's length helps the sinking fly line sink it and the fly.

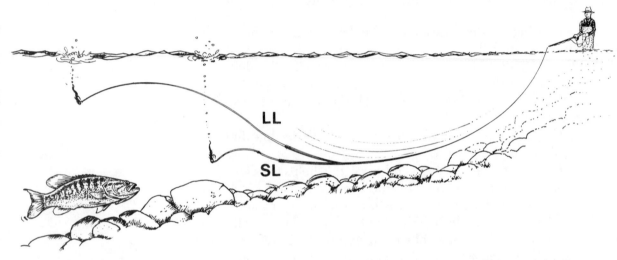

The effect of leader length on a sinking line and fly if flies and line strike the water at the same moment. LL—the long leader inhibits sinking. SL—the short leader has little effect on the sink rate.

Bass seem untroubled by shorter leaders, especially if they have a long tip section, twenty-four to thirty-six inches. Most bass waters are laden with algae or plant stems so these fish generally ignore the leader and line tip.

You can buy special six-foot knotless tapered leaders or cut a foot or so off the standard knotless tapered 7½-foot leader butt section and have a reasonable substitute. If you should need a sinking-line leader shorter than four feet, a simple level leader will work nicely.

Level or knotted tapered leaders do not function as well as the knotless taper for bass fishing. Their one advantage is that you can make them by yourself. If knotless tapers are not available or are too expensive for you, then by tying sections of leader material together you can create a reasonable substitute.

The new braided-butt tapered leaders are supposed to be the answer for an expensive shortcut to excellent fly presentation. For typical bass fly fishing they are impractical and unduly expensive. Though they cast and present a bass fly fairly well, they soon fail because they do not hold up well for the stresses and abuse a bass leader takes daily.

Fly-line backing is a braided Dacron or nylon line that is connected to the tail end of the fly line and the fly reel. It serves three purposes:

It provides reserve line when a big fish pulls off more than the entire length of the fly line;

It fills the reel spool up to a point where fly line can be most efficiently wound back on the reel. A full reel spool also is less likely to tangle or backlash when fly line is pulled off by fisher or fish; and

Braided Backing

It fills the spool to a larger diameter so fly line wound on after it will have less tendency to coil and will straighten, cast, and fish better.

You should have at least fifty yards of backing on any fly reel that you bass fish with and 100 to 200 yards is not excessive if your reel will hold it and the fly line! *Always use braided Dacron or nylon for backing*. It should be twenty to thirty-pound test so it will not break before the leader tip at the fly should a strong fish or other circumstance pull it all off the reel. *Never use monofilament nylon for backing;* this tangles over or under itself on the spool and by stretching can cause swelling damage to the reel spool.

Bass usually do not make long fast runs like big salmon, steelhead, stripers, barracuda, or bonefish—though sometimes they do. Or you may hook a big striper, snook, or muskie that will require reserve backing. Good braided backing will last many years; it will always be good insurance and will make your reel operate more efficiently.

THE FLY REEL

The primary function of the fly reel is to hold the fly-line components. Unlike conventional lure-casting tools, the fly reel does not cast or retrieve lures—

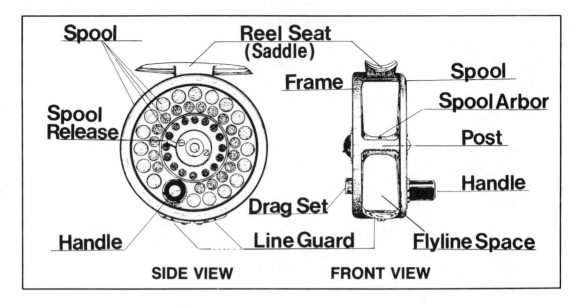

Spool | **Reel Seat** (Saddle) | **Frame** | **Spool** | **Spool Arbor** | **Post** | **Handle**

Spool Release

Handle | **Drag Set** | **Line Guard** | **Flyline Space**

SIDE VIEW | **FRONT VIEW**

The parts of a fly reel.

though it *can* be used to retrieve fly line once a fish is hooked or to play out fly line and backing if the fish swims strongly away.

The fly reel may also be equipped with one or more adjustable "drag" devices that make the fish work hard and tire out quicker when it pulls line off the spool.

Because of its function on one-handed fly rods, the fly reel is always positioned *behind* the rod's handle and hangs *below or under* the handle.

(Below Left) **Three types of fly reels** 1. Single action 2. Multiplier 3. Automatic

(Below Right) A fly reel with extra spools for the three basic bass fly lines: floating, sink-tip, and sinking.

Many fly reels have extra spools available so you can quickly change to a different fly line as fishing circumstances change. Such spools cost less than another reel and provide an efficient method for using different fly lines as needed. Most spools remove from the reel frame by a simple finger press of a lever or button release on the spool's face.

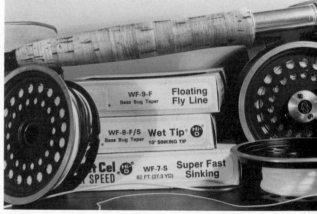

There are three basic fly-reel designs.

Single action—a simple direct-drive one-to-one ratio winch. One revolution of the reel's handle causes the reel spool to make one complete revolution. This is the most popular type because of its simple, trouble-free design. It's also available in a wide range of prices, sizes, drags, options, and extra-spool options.

Multiplier fly reel—has a similar size, shape, and design as the single action but with a complex gear winch that allows 1 to 1½, 2, 2⅓ or 3 retrieve ratios for faster retrieves than the single-action reel. Though not as popular, they are available with the same actions as single action, especially in sizes and extra spools. The multiplier has the best design because it incorporates the best features of both the single-action and automatic reel.

Automatic fly reel—has a flat coil-spring design that allows you to retrieve fly line automatically. It operates on the same principle as a typical pull-down window shade. When the line is pulled off the reel, an internal flat coil spring next to the spool is wound tighter. When the spring tension is released by pressing down on a button or handle, the spring uncoils and winds line onto the spool. This provides effortless retrieving of a *limited* amount of line. Because the spring is winding tighter as you pull line off the reel spool, there is excessive tension on the spool that makes pulling line off by the fisherman or fish difficult. Automatic reels are the least popular fly reel due to their limited spool capacity, drag restrictions, heavy weight, lack of extra spools and lack of mechanical dependability.

These reels have been popular in the South for bass and panfishing because they can retrieve slack line quickly and maintain tension on the line when a small bass or panfish hits. But the reel limits versatility with modern bass-fishing techniques. Automatic reels are most helpful to fly fishermen with limited use of one hand, since they allow you to hold the rod and retrieve with just one hand.

MODERN BASS FLY-REEL REQUIREMENTS

The best fly reels for bass will have a large-capacity spool to hold a large fly-line size (7 to 10-weight) plus ample backing. The larger spool permits rapid retrieves of fly line and backing. Whenever in doubt about reel size, pick the larger model. This will hold a larger range of fly-line sizes and more backing. It will retrieve line and backing faster and with more power. Larger fly reels tend to be sturdier and more durable than smaller models. Don't be concerned with an extra ounce or two of weight; the fly reel is positioned like a counter-balance to the rod and working fly line, and a heavier reel will be *less* tiring than lighter fly reels on hand and wrist during prolonged fishing.

The best reels will have an adjustable drag system and hand-operated reel-spool rim drag. They will pro-vide a fast retrieve ratio. Extra spools are a definite plus. A light-weight but durable corrosion-resistant construction is needed for most boat and wading condi-tions. Finally, the reel should have an easily convertible right or left-hand reel option.

The multiplier is the best choice for most bass fly fishing. The second most practical choice is the single action. If you also plan to use the reel for larger and long-running species such as snook, bluefish, redfish, tarpon, and bonefish, the single action with good disc drag would be a better choice than the multiplier. The automatic serves decently only for bass and panfish fly fishers who use one fly line and do not expect to catch bass or panfish larger than two or three pounds.

THE FLY ROD

The fly rod is the most symbolic part of the fly-tackle system even though the fly line is its key component. Fly rods are typically longer than most other bass-fish-ing rods; they appear to be very slender, delicate, and graceful instruments, but fly rods vary greatly in strength and design according to their specific purpose. Primarily, the fly rod is a tool that makes your arm and hand more efficient for casting flies, placing them prop-erly and accurately, and making them move enticingly; it enables you to set the hook, then maintain pressure on the fish until it is tired and positioned for capture. Per hour fished, the fly rod will let you make more casts than other lure methods.

Since line control is so crucial in fly fishing, the long rod is of prime importance. The rod's length, material, composition, taper, line-size capability, and component

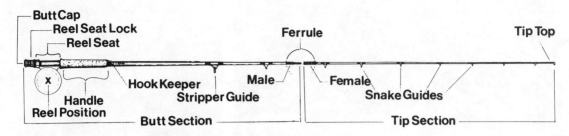

Fly rod parts

fittings all determine the rod's potential for a particular type of fly fishing. Fly rods specifically made for bass are a more or less recent and—very welcome—development.

Fly-rod components. Fly rods have three general parts—butt, midsection, and tip. The butt is the thickest, stiffest part of the rod; it contains the handle and provides leverage and strength to the rod. The midsection supplies the rod's casting action and power. And the tip, the smallest part of the rod, absorbs the shock of casting, striking a fish, setting the hook, and playing the fish.

The rod may be one piece, but to facilitate carrying and storing, most fly rods are made in two, three, or more sections.

The *fly rod handle* has two functions. It securely holds the fly reel to the rod and provides a grip for holding the rod. This handle, which is usually made of cork, provides a smooth firm grip for the fly fisher's casting hand. (The best grip shape for bass is illustrated.)

The *fly-reel seat* provides a base to which the fly reel can be attached. There are three general types of seats—double or single slip ring, downscrew-locking, and upscrew-locking. All three do a nice job of holding the fly reel to the rod but the uplocking fly reel seat is best for bass fly fishing.

The handle may have an extension to the rear of the reel seat called an extension or a fighting butt.

Just in front of most fly-rod handles is a small wire ring or loop through which you place the fly hook when storing the assembled fly tackle. This keeper holds the fly next to the fly rod so the fly is less likely to hook you or other objects. Line guides may also be used for this purpose.

The *guides* on a fly rod serve to hold the fly line close to the rod for efficient control when casting and fishing.

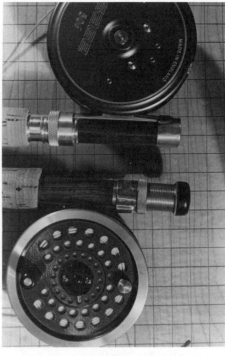

Four Types of Single-Handed Reel Seats (right to left)

1. Slip rings 2. Down-locking screw 3. Up-locking screw 4. Up-locking with extension butt—the most functional for bass fly fishing.

Detail of two types of screw-locking reel seats: 1. (Bottom) Up-locking— the most functional; it allows the hand to avoid the reel-seat metal and has a short extension butt that helps protect the fly reel when resting on the floor or ground and gives leverage to arm and wrist. 2. Down-locking (top)

Each guide's size and placement is precisely chosen to complement all casting and fishing functions. The stripper guide is the first large guide above the handle. It is designed to reduce fly-line friction and wear, and to control line pulled off the reel. Snake guides are small, simple, lightweight wires that resemble a tiny snake; they're located on the mid and tip sections of the rod. The top guide is a closed-loop guide on the tip of the fly rod.

In order to store or transport fly rods that are seven to ten feet long, most fly rods are made in two or more sections and are joined and held together by simple ferrules. Two ferrule parts, male and female, are built into rod sections and when joined provide a smooth slip-proof connection in harmony with the fly rod's flexibility.

All modern fly rods will have specifications on the rod butt or on the butt plate of the handle. This will indicate the best fly-line weight the rod is designed to cast, the length of the rod, the rod model code, and the weight of the rod.

Fly-Line Weight This Rod is Designed to Cast

Fly-Rod Length

908 · 9ft. for 8weight Flylines   3¾oz

**Rod Model Code
(i.e., 9 feet, for 8-weight line)**

Fly-Rod Weight

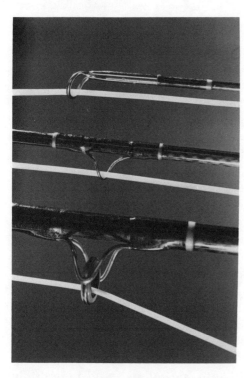

Fly-Rod Guides

Tip-top guide

Snake guide

Stripper guide

Fly rods are manufactured with specifications that allow you to choose the correct rod for your use or needs. The most important is the fly-line weight, which is printed—with the rod's length and weight—on the butt section near the rod handle of most fly rods.

If the rod comes with a cloth case and/or storage tube this information should also be printed on it.

Fly-Rod Materials. Today's fly rods are manufactured with one or more combinations of bamboo cane, fiberglass, carbon fiber, boron filament, or Kevlar. All of these materials when properly used make excellent fly rods but each will have a particular feel, performance, and weight.

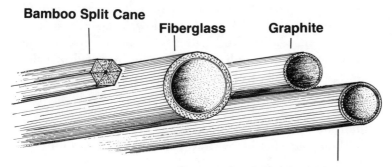

Bamboo Split Cane

Fiberglass **Graphite**

Composite Graphite-Boron Kevlar

Four major fly-rod blanks. Bamboo, fiberglass, graphite, and graphite/boron/Kevlar—with the diameters in perspective for a single fly-line weight size.

Bamboo and fiberglass are generally heavier and less efficient than boron, graphite, and Kevlar. Tubular rods of graphite, composites of graphite and boron or graphite, boron, and Kevlar are best for bass fly fishing.

Fly-Rod Lengths. Practical fly-rod lengths range between 6½ to fourteen feet. Rods shorter than ten feet are considered to be one-handed rods and those longer than 10½ feet are best cast with two hands. Short fly rods (6½ to 7½ feet) generally are best for fly fishing restricted areas such as small bushy or tree-canopied creeks. Shorter fly rods generally use lighter line weights (2 to 5) and are best for small flies. Fly rods between eight and nine feet are excellent for typical lakes, ponds, streams, and rivers. These lengths are most practical, too, for casting and controlling a wide range of flies. Eight and a half feet is probably the best all-around length for the widest variety of uses.

Fly rods in excess of nine feet are principally for long casts and extra line control. As fly rods get longer they become more sensitive to control and tend to multiply poor casting habits. They also become more tiring to use because they are larger and heavier.

Fly-Rod Actions. Fly-rod performance is usually understood to be its action when casting or being flexed. Fly-rod action is probably the most discussed, cussed-and-fussed-about subject in fly fishing when fly fishers gather. Action is influenced by the rod's material, taper design, length, ferrules, and guides. It is also modified by how much loading or weight the fly line and fly put on it might exert. Unfortunately, manufacturers do not always identify actions clearly on the rod.

Some fly rods are described according to the rod's purpose—dry fly, streamer, or bug rod. These descriptions simply mean this rod's design and action cast those type flies best.

Since each of us has different reflexes and coordination, a particular fly-rod action may best complement your special ability. If you have slow, relaxed reflexes, initially you will do well with a slow-action rod; if you react quickly to stimuli, the fast-action rod will initially feel best for you. But as you become a good fly caster you will probably become interested in doing more specific types of fly fishing. To do these best may require a different action fly rod than what is "natural" for you. By then you should be able to adjust to the different actions required.

There are three main fly-rod actions:

Slow (soft)—under specific fly-line weight, this rod is designed to have a full progressive curve from rod tip to rod handle. When a slow-flexed rod is allowed to straighten, it does so with a fairly slow movement compared to that of a fast-action rod. This produces slow fly-line speed and wide fly-line loops;

Medium—under specific fly-line weight, this rod is designed for less rod flex in the butt section than the slow-action rod. It produces medium line speed and fairly tight line loop shape;

Fast—under specific fly-line weights, this rod is designed to flex very little in the butt and midsection and moderately in the tip. It produces the fastest moving fly-line speed and small or tight fly line loops.

You will find many variations of these three basic actions but for convenience this simple system works well.

Note: Fly lines heavier than what the rod is designed for will make it feel like a slower model; fly lines lighter than the rod is designed for will make it seem faster.

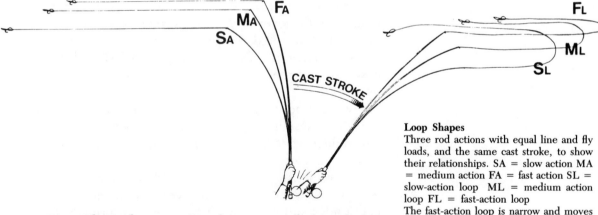

Loop Shapes
Three rod actions with equal line and fly loads, and the same cast stroke, to show their relationships. SA = slow action MA = medium action FA = fast action SL = slow-action loop ML = medium action loop FL = fast-action loop
The fast-action loop is narrow and moves the fly faster and farther.

Bass Fly-Rod Action. At first it was believed that bass fly rods performed best if they had a very slow action and were made for line weights of 9, 10, 11, or 12. The slower-action bamboo and glass rods used then required slower moving lines with wider, more wind-resistant line loop shapes. *So the extra-heavy lines did most of the casting work with excessive momentum rather efficiently.* Such fly rods were coarse and heavy, and little fun to catch bass on—certainly one reason many of us did not fall in love with bass bugging.

Today, fly rods cast and fish bass flies best if they have medium-fast or fast actions with 7, 8, and 9-weight lines. This is because such rods, especially graphite and boron, cast the larger, more wind-resistant and heavy bass flies with tighter loops and higher speed. These lighter, extra-sensitive, smaller, fast-action bass fly rods are delightful to cast and catch bass on. They make bass fly fishing as sporting as any trout or salmon fishing.

The Bass Fly Rod. Any fly rod between 6½ and 10 feet that will cast a 5 to 12-weight fly line can be used to fly fish for bass; but you should know which rod works best for this kind of fishing.

Line weights—7, 8, 9-weight; 8 is the best all-around choice. Most modern graphite/boron rods will handle two line weights and are generally advertised to perform with these.

Rod lengths—lengths of eight, 8½, 8¾, and nine feet. The 8¾ feet is the best choice length.

Rod action and design—a medium-fast or fast-action graphite or graphite/boron rod with an extra-powerful butt and handle section is ideal. This bass rod must pick up and cast the fly line with maximum speed. It will help animate the fly and strike extremely well. It will have power and backbone to drive a large hook into a tough mouth, lever and stop a strong bass from diving under structure and escaping.

The rod handle should be equipped with a strong down-locking reel seat and a one or two-inch extension butt.

Fly-rod guides should be of the large heavy-duty variety for minimum fly-line friction resistance; this will also reduce your false casting and allow longer fly line shoots.

The rod finish and/or walls should be durable, to protect the rod from many hazards common to bass fly fishing; guides and wraps must be strong, to protect them from damage. This will protect the rod against banging on bass boats, jerking flies out of tree limbs, striking objects while casting, and similar hard use.

BALANCED BASS FLY TACKLE

A "balanced fly-tackle outfit," a phrase often used in fly fishing, seems to infer to a newcomer that the fly rod and reel balance in your hand. Not so. Balance means that the rod/line/leader/fly are correctly calibrated to cast and fish properly together. Example: a 7-weight, bass-bug-taper fly line should be cast with a rod made to cast a 7-weight fly line. The proper choice of leader and fly must complement these two 7-weight components. Most modern fly rods have the necessary information printed on their butt sections. Reel balance means mostly that the reel is the correct size to hold the proper fly line and needed backing.

Today most fly-tackle stores and mail-order catalogs offer balanced fly-tackle outfits on request or will match components for you. These often include the fly rod, fly reel with backing, fly line, and leader attached. Many tackle stores and catalogs will also sell you extra reel spools "loaded" with extra fly lines you might need, such as sink-tip and full-sinking lines.

BASS FLY-TACKLE-OUTFIT SELECTIONS

Here are some outfits that will get you started. They need not be expensive. Most balanced trout, salmon, or saltwater fly outfits will work. But it may be more rewarding to begin with correctly balanced bass fly tackle; this will help you learn faster.

If I had to pick one outfit to bass fly fish and enjoy the widest range of opportunities, this would be my choice:

Fly rod—7 to 8-weight, 8¾ feet medium-fast action, graphite/boron composite with extra-strong butt section. The rod handle, with uplocking reel seat, should be equipped with a two-inch extension butt.

Fly reel—2½-to-1 multiplier reel with large enough spool to hold an 8-weight floating weight-forward bug-taper line and 150 yards of thirty-pound-test backing, with one or two extra reel spools.

Fly lines and leaders (listed in priority):

1. WF8F bug taper and bass bug nine-foot knotless tapered leader with twelve- or fourteen-pound-test tip.

2. WF7F (standard) taper and six-foot knotless, tapered sinking leader with twelve-pound-test tip.

3. WF7S (extra-fast-sinking) and four-foot knotless tapered or level leader with fourteen-pound-test tip.

These three choices allow you to cover all areas bass live in with the widest range of dry, floating, diving, sinking/swimming, and bottom-hopping flies from size 10 to 3/0. Note that I have selected an 8-weight floating line but 7-weight sinking fly lines. If a fly rod is made to cast two line weights, the floating line will cast best in the heavier weight and the sinking line in the lighter weight. Regarding choice 3: the full-sinking is probably the least important but 1 and 2 are needed to cover bass waters best. I use these three line systems at a ratio of floating—60%, sinking tip—30%, and full-sinking—10% on an annual four-season bass-fly-fishing cycle.

PANFISH AND LIGHT BASS OUTFITS

For panfish and small-to-medium bass, particularly in ponds, small lakes, and streams, I recommend the outfits listed; they will cast and fish flies in hook sizes 14 to 2 well.

Fly rod—6 or 7-weight, 8½-foot medium-fast action graphite rod with uplocking reel seat. The butt should be fairly stiff.

Fly reel—2½-to-1 ratio multiplier or single action, large enough to hold a 7-weight WF floating line and 100 yards of twenty-pound-test backing.

Fly lines—these two will work well: WF7F bass-bug floating line with a 7½ or nine-foot knotless tapered butt or heavy-butt leader; tip strength should be eight-to-ten pound test. Or, WF6F/S—fast-sinking tip with 6-foot knotless taper, ten-pound-test tip. I usually cut four or five feet off this sinking-tip fly line for better casting and fishing results with this lighter outfit.

MEDIUM-HEAVY BASS OUTFIT

This outfit is ideal for large bass and associated species in large lakes, large rivers, and brackish-water canals and bays. For casting and fishing bass flies from sizes 4 to 5/0.

Fly rod—8 or 9-weight, nine-foot fast-action graphite/boron composite with powerful butt, uplocking reel seat, and two-inch extension or fighting butt.

Fly reel—2½-to-1 heavy-duty multiplier or single action with sturdy disc-drag system. The rod should be

large enough to hold WF9F bug floating fly line and 200 yards of thirty-pound-test backing.

Fly lines:

WF9F saltwater or bug floating fly line with a heavy-butt knotless tapered leader and a fourteen to eighteen-pound-test tip;

WF8S/F ten-foot extra-fast sink-tip with six-foot sinking line, knotless tapered leader, and a fourteen to sixteen-pound-test tip.

ST8F—extra hi-speed sinking thirty-foot head with a four-foot knotless tapered or level leader and a fourteen to sixteen-pound test tip.

EXTRA-HEAVY DUTY BASS-FLY FISHING OUTFIT

For large southern or Florida bass, peacock bass, stripers, or brackish-water snook and tarpon, redfish, or places where surface and underwater structures create extreme casting and fishing obstacles and hazards, I recommend this outfit, which casts and fishes fly sizes 4 to 6/0.

Fly rod—10 to 11-weight, eight foot, extra-fast action graphite/boron composite rod with heavy-duty, extra-stiff butt and midsection, an uplocking reel seat, two-inch-wide base extension butt, and extra-heavy-gauge guides and wraps.

Fly reel—heavy-duty anti-reverse single-action reel with a powerful disc drag and enough spool capacity to hold WF11-weight fly line plus 200 yards of thirty-pound-test backing.

Fly line/Leaders:

WF11F saltwater or bug floating line with about one half of the line's tip-taper cut off. The leader should be 7½-foot heavy-butt knotless tapered, with fourteen to twenty-pound-test tip or 7½-foot level mono of twenty to sixty-pound-test for bite or cutoff protection.

WF10F/S extra-fast-sinking ten-foot tip with six-foot level or tapered leader, tip test sixteen to twenty-pound, or equipped with thirty to sixty-pound mono-bite tippet.

3
Tackle Assembly

It's easy to assemble bass fly tackle properly and doing so will promote much faster success. First, you must learn the knots and connections of the fly-line system and next how to assemble the components and prepare them correctly for fishing.

Fly-line components with the five knots that connect them.

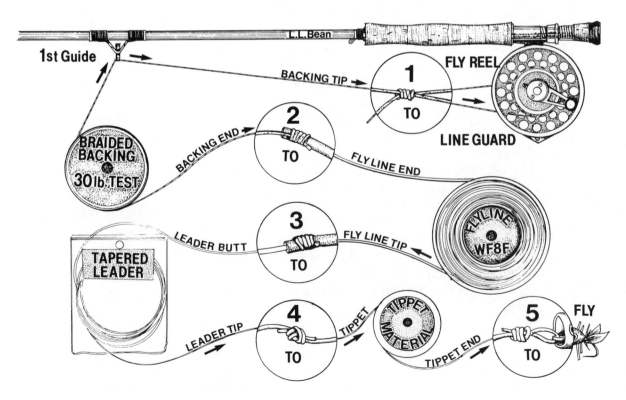

FLY-LINE SYSTEM COMPONENT ASSEMBLY

Connecting the fly-line system with strong, easy-to-make, and small, smooth junctions is absolutely necessary for high performance. Since the fly line is so large, knotting it causes too bulky a connection to pass smoothly through the rod guides—and one that can catch easily on water objects. The ideal fly-line connection must include fixing the backing or leader to the fly line. The connections I use are the best yet developed; they're neat, strong, and easy to do yourself.

Study the diagram. Notice that there are six parts to this system: the fly reel, braided backing, fly line, leader, leader tippet, and fly. To join these parts efficiently, there are at least four connections, five if you include the addition of the tippet to the tip end of the leader. Of these, note that the same knot—the Duncan Loop or Uni-knot—can be used to make four of the fly-line connections. As shown, they are: 1. Backing to fly reel; 2. Backing to fly line; 3. Leader butt to fly line; 4. Leader tippet to leader; and 5. Tippet end to fly.

To set up your system, select a well-lighted table-top surface and comfortable chair. Have on hand a small pair of needle-nose pliers with smooth jaws, scissors, fingernail clippers, several size 8 to 10 darning needles and needle vise, or an L. L. Bean Knot Tool Kit, and an emery stone. Have ready your fly rod's handle section, fly reel, spool of backing, fly line, leader, tippet material, and a large bass fly.

Make sure your reel's click brake or drag system is set to operate correctly when used with the hand you intend to hold the reel's handle with. Most new single-action or multiplier fly reels are convertible to right or left-hand winding and drag systems. They usually come from the manufacturer set up to operate with right-hand cranking. If you wish to use the other hand, refer to the instructions included or ask a knowledgeable friend or salesperson to help you convert the reel. I strongly recommend you use the hand you do *not* cast with to control the fly reel—that is, if you cast right-handed, use your left hand for retrieving. With this arrangement you do not have to switch hands after you cast, to begin fighting the fish or retrieving the fly line.

Place the fly reel on the fly-rod handle. Make sure that the reel handle is on the side you intend to use for retrieve and that the reel's line guard is positioned for-ward. If not, remove the retaining screws and place it forward. This will provide a convenient handle for the reel while you wind on the backing.

From the spool of backing, remove five or six feet of line and place its tag end down through the stripper guide toward the handle, then through the reel's line guard and around the fly reel's spool spindle. Make sure the backing end passes in and out at the same place and not between one or two of the reel's frame posts; if you do the latter, you'll find it's impossible to tie the line to the spool. Pull at least twelve inches of backing through the reel; this will be enough with which to tie the Duncan Loop. (See diagram "Backing to Fly Reel.") *Be sure you snug the knot tightly down on the spool's spindle; it must not slip on it.*

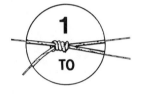

Knot #1 Backing to Fly Reel/Duncan Loop or Uni-Knot

1. Pass the backing line through the line guard of the reel and then around the reel spool and back out of the line guard—with eight to twelve inches of tag end remaining to tie the knot with.
2. Form a large loop with the tag end to-ward, then away from, the reel.
3. The tag excess should be about six to eight inches now.
4. With the tag end, make five wraps away from the reel, through the loop and standing line, as shown here.
5. Pull on the tag to tighten the knot over the line
6. Pull hard on the line to slide and tighten the loop against the spool spin-dle of the reel. Clip the excess tag end off. Make sure that the knot loop is ab-solutely tight against the spindle.

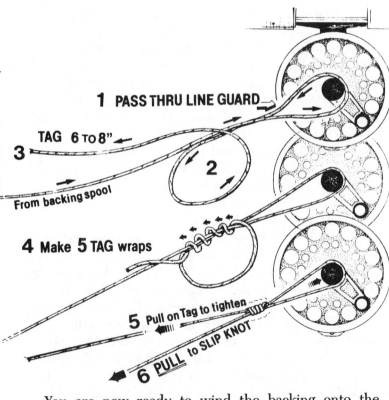

You are now ready to wind the backing onto the spool. Place a pencil, pen, or wooden dowel through the center hole of the backing spool. Have someone hold the backing spool by the pencil as you reel backing onto the reel's spool; if alone, place the pencil between your knees for control and tension. *Always wind the handle in a forward, down, back, and up motion.* This would be clockwise with your right and counter-clockwise with your left hand. Use just enough tension between backing spool and reel spool to ensure that the backing is firmly wrapped on the fly-reel spool.

As you wind backing on, try to position the consecutive winds on the spool evenly, going from one side to the other and back. Use your rod hand's index finger to control tension and position the backing on the spool.

You should fill the reel's spool with this backing to a level that allows the right amount of reserve space to hold the fly line and still have a finger tip's clearance between the reel post and fly line. This may be hard to judge. If you're in doubt you can always put too much on and adjust it by removing some if the fly line is crowded. Also you can ask an experienced fly-fishing friend or your tackle dealer how much backing is needed to fill your particular reel with the fly line you have. Clearly, a floating line will take up more reel spool space than the same weight and length sinking line because it is so much larger in diameter.

After backing is placed on the fly reel, you'll need to attach the fly line to the backing. If the fly line is wound directly onto the plastic spool, find the end and pull off about twenty-four inches of fly line. If the fly line is only loosely coiled around the plastic spool, carefully remove the two or three twist-on wires, then find the end and pull out the fly line length. The manufacturer will usually include in the container the directions for unspooling the fly line. If you use a weight-forward line, you must tie the backing to the back or shooting portion of the fly line. There is usually a small printed tab placed on the correct end by the manufacturer that identifies this end. For level or double-taper fly lines it does not matter which end you use first.

To attach the backing to the fly line's end, follow the "Backing to the Fly Line" diagram, which is simply a modification of the "Backing to Fly Reel" knot.

Once you've attached the backing to the fly line, use the same technique you used with the backing—carefully wind the fly line onto the reel spool. Leave about four feet of fly line loose off the reel for the leader to fly-line connection. Should your reel spool be too full of backing to accept the entire fly line and still have room to put the end of your little finger between it and the reel's frame posts, you must do one of two things: Remove the fly line, cut the backing-to-fly-line knot, and

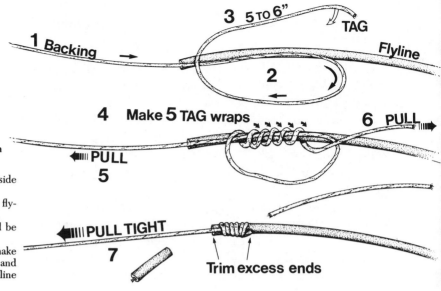

1 Backing →

3 5 TO 6"   TAG   Flyline

2

4 Make **5** TAG wraps   **6** PULL →

PULL **5**

PULL TIGHT **7**   Trim excess ends

Knot #2 Backing to Fly Line/Duncan Loop

1. Lay ten inches of backing alongside the end of the fly line.
2. Loop the tag end back toward the fly-line end to form a two-inch loop.
3. The tag end of the backing should be five or six inches long.
4. With the tag end of the backing, make five wraps over the fly line and through the loop back from the fly-line end.
5. Grasp the fly line and wraps, then carefully pull on the backing to close the slack in the loop. Take care not to allow the knot to slip off the end of the fly line.
6. Pull on the tag end to tighten the knot wraps and loop firmly against the end of the fly line. Try to keep the knot wraps close together but not overlapping.
7. Pull the backing tight and trim the excess fly line and backing so that you have a neat trouble-free knot. Coat the knot and fly-line end with a flexible waterproof cement to make the connection smoother and stronger.

remove some part of the backing so that the fly line will fit the spool; or, if you are putting on a level or weight-forward fly line, you can cut off as much as ten to fifteen feet without affecting in any way the fly line's performance in bass fishing. The advantage of the last adjustment is that it allows more backing to be kept.

If the leader is coiled and stored in a package, remove it carefully. Place three or four fingers inside the leader coils and spread your fingers to maintain a firm tension on the leader coils. With your other hand, carefully unravel the leader while maintaining finger tension on the remaining coils until the leader is completely uncoiled. This simple procedure will prevent some time-consuming tangles. With your hands, stretch and stroke the leader's butt section to remove some of the coil memory of the nylon. This makes tying it to the fly line much faster and easier.

Attach the leader's butt to the fly-line tip by following the steps in the "Leader to Fly Line" illustration. Note that there is an option to the Duncan Loop Knot included. This is a special leader-to-fly-line connection that, when properly done, gives you a simple, smooth, and strong alternative. There are several gadgets for attaching the leader to the fly line that you should be advised against. I don't recommend using the metal-wire eyelet with a barbed point fly-line connection or plastic fly-line/leader connections for bass fly fishing. These are apt to fail. Either of these recommended connections takes about the same time to do as using the gadgets—and they're much more dependable and efficient.

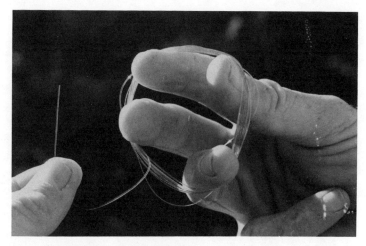

Uncoiling leaders. To avoid tangling a new tapered leader when you uncoil it, simply place your fingers through the loop coils and maintain tension as you unwrap it.

Knot #3 Leader to Fly Line/Duncan Loop

For knotless tapered leaders—before tippet is added or with tippet removed and hollow-core fly lines.

1. Begin with a size 12 or 10 beading, darning, or extra-small sewing-machine needle.
2. Insert the eyed needle end into the core of the fly-line's tip ½ to ⅜ of an inch; then push it out the side of the coating, as shown.
3. Pass the leader tip through the eye of the needle. If the tip is too large, shave one or two inches of it with a razor blade until it is small enough to pass through the eye.
4. Pull the needle and end of the leader out of the tip of the fly line.
5. Pull the leader through to about six or eight inches from the end of the butt.
6. With the end of the butt, form a loop next to the fly line, away from the tip end of the line.
7. Holding the fly line and loop firmly, make four snug, close-spaced wraps beginning at the exit hole, around the fly line, and through the loop, as shown. Make sure that you wrap the leader butt away from the fly line tip end.
8. Take great care to keep the leader-butt wraps held tightly in place while the leader is pulled to snug up the knot's loop.
9. Make one more extra-hard pull on the leader to snug it completely; then trim the excess leader-butt tag close to the knot. To make the knot smoother, coat it and the tip of the line with a fast-drying flexible, waterproof cement.

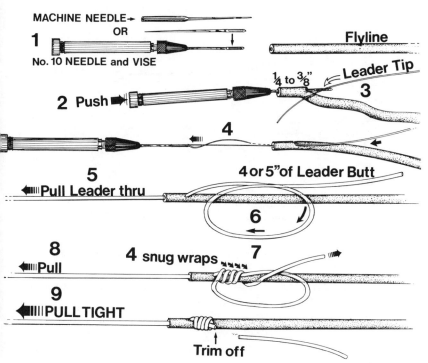

MACHINE NEEDLE→
OR
1 No. 10 NEEDLE and VISE

Flyline

2 Push →

¼ to ⅜" ← **Leader Tip**
3

4

5 ← Pull Leader thru

4 or 5"of Leader Butt

6

8 ← Pull **4 snug wraps** **7**

9 ← PULL TIGHT

↑ **Trim off**

Note: If you have a knotted tapered leader, first pass the needle *point* through the core of the fly line and out the side. Now, with a double-edge razor blade, shave three inches of the leader's butt end, so it will pass through the needle's eye exit. Now pull needle and leader butt through exit hole. Now follow the instructions for Knot #3, beginning with steps 5 and 6.

Note: Other leader-to-fly-line options: If your line has a solid core, such as lead core, monofilament, or twisted filament, tie the leader to this with Knot #2 (Backing to Fly Line).

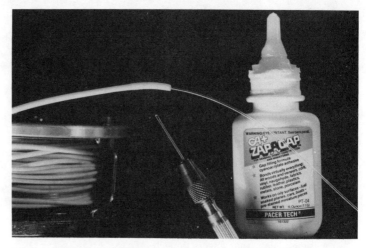

A near-perfect fly-line/leader connection can be made simply and quickly with the new bonding agent Zap a Gap and a needle vise.

Splicing the leader and fly line together with Zap a Gap is a no-knot option to using Knot #3. This glue has been thoroughly tested for superior waterproof bonding between nylon monofilament leader and fly lines. Properly bonded, the fly line or leader butt will break before the connection will fail.

1. Insert the eye of a size 10 or 12 beading or darning needle into the fly-line tip's core.
2. Push the needle half an inch up inside the fly-line core, then out the side of the coating.
3. Insert an inch of knotless leader tip (whose butt end has been straightened) through the needle eye.
4. Now pull needle and leader tip out of the fly-line tip.
5. Remove needle and pull knotless leader after tip until only three or four inches of butt remain outside of the needle hole.
6. Using 50 to 100-grit sandpaper, thoroughly roughen a half-inch section of the leader's butt next to the fly-line tip. *Note:* If leader-butt end has been straightened, the line/leader connection will also be straight.
7. Place a small drop of Zap a Gap on the roughed section and spread the glue evenly over it with the nozzle of the glue bottle. *Move immediately to next step.*
8. Now quickly grip the exposed leader-butt end with pliers or forceps and, holding the fly-line tip with a firm grip, give a quick, short pull on the leader-butt end to pull the roughed section just inside the fly line.
9. Allow fifteen to twenty seconds for the Zap a Gap glue to cure and form a permanent bond. Trim off the exposed excess butt end flush with the fly-line coating. After trimming, give a few sharp tugs on the leader butt and fly line to test the bond. Pull the end of the trimmed butt into the fly-line finish for a smooth coating surface. *Note:* A small excess of glue may remain at the fly-line tip. If you allow this to dry for about thirty minutes it will provide a smoother link at the junction of fly-line tip and leader butt. The glue drying may be accelerated to ten seconds if you apply a catalyst called Zip-Kicker. Zap a Gap is available at the L.L. Bean Freeport Store and through the L.L. Bean mailorder catalog, as well as at fly fishing and hardware stores and hobby shops; it is wholesale distributed through Wapsi Fly Co., Rt. 5, Box 57-E, Mountain Home, AR 72653.

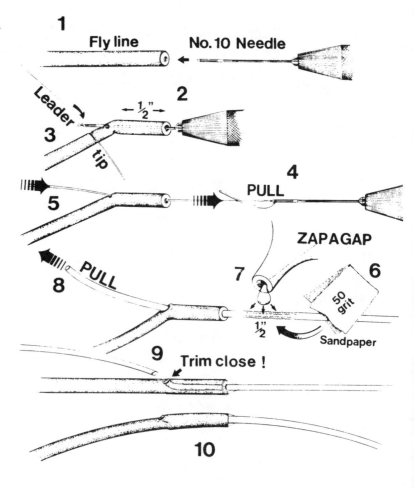

For optimum casting performance, the fly-line tip and leader-butt junction should be of the same general flexibility. Bass leaders usually are designed with butts that match the 7, 8, 9, and 10-weight line tips. If your connection is too stiff, here's what to do to make it match: stroke it with a smooth-jawed pair of needle-nose pliers to flatten the leader slightly. This will make the butt more flexible—to match the fly-line tip.

For connecting two sections of nylon monofilament line, whether for making a knotted tapered leader or tying leader tip to tippet, the surgeon's knot is superior to the popular blood or barrel knot. It is stronger, smaller, faster, and much easier to tie, and less sensitive to size or hardness mismatches. Practice this knot on level tippet material of ten to twelve-pound-test before using it on your tapered leader tip.

It's good practice to add a tippet section to your new knotless tapered leader before you use it. About fifteen to eighteen inches is ideal. This addition only requires one small, dependable surgeon's knot and it will significantly prolong your leader's life for two reasons: tying on flies uses inexpensive tippet not expensive leaders. Tying on a fly with a Duncan loop knot will use up three to six inches of material each time you change flies. Second, most leader damage, especially due to abrasion or "wind knots," occurs on the twelve inches

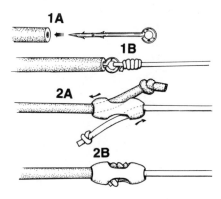

Gadget Leader-to-Fly Line Connectors

1A. Fly-line tip, metal-barbed eyelet.
1B. Eyelet is inserted into fly-line core and leader butt is tied to eye with a secure knot.
2A. Fly line, plastic leader connector. Pass end of fly line through end and side of connector and place an overhand knot in it. Do the same with leader's butt on opposite end.
2B. Now pull both line and leader knots inside the connector and clip any excess ends off.

Knot #4 Tippet to Leader— Surgeon's Knot

1. Place leader tip and tippet section ends side by side in opposite directions, overlapping about five to seven inches each.
2. With them together, form a two-inch diameter common loop and pass the leader tip tag and tippet's long end through the loop.
3. Pass both through the loop once more. Wet the loop wraps with your lips.
4. Tighten knot by first pulling on long sides of leader and tippet, then on tag ends. Trim excess tag ends. *Note:* If you are tying together two different types of nylon, it is best to make a third pass with both through the loop to avoid having the harder type cutting the softer type.

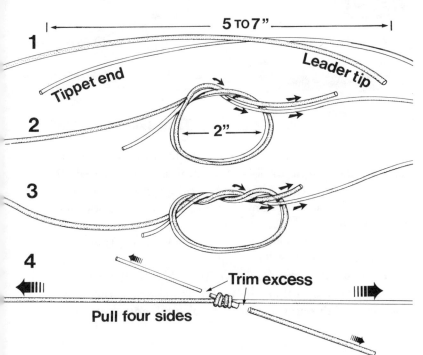

or so of your leader next to the fly. So the tippet really reduces these wear problems on the main leader significantly. Your leader will last about four times longer than without the tippet.

FLY-TO-LEADER ATTACHMENT— THE DUNCAN LOOP OR UNI-KNOT

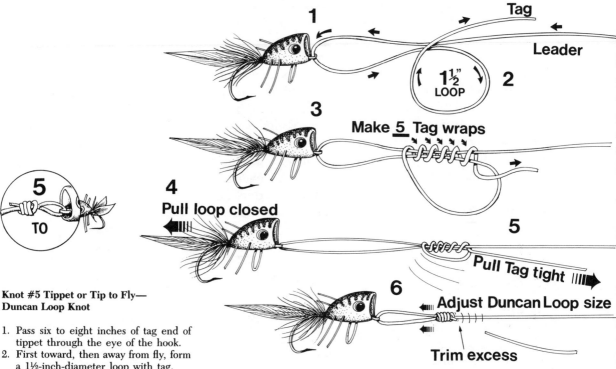

Knot #5 Tippet or Tip to Fly— Duncan Loop Knot

1. Pass six to eight inches of tag end of tippet through the eye of the hook.
2. First toward, then away from fly, form a 1½-inch-diameter loop with tag.
3. Pass tag through and around loop and tippet five times; make sure wraps are away from fly.
4. Wet the wraps with your lips and snug five wraps by holding onto tag and pulling fly as illustrated.
5. Tighten knot by pulling very tightly on tag end. Degree of tightening determines how knot will slide on tippet for keeping the loop open or slipping it closed. If you are using a heavy tippet, over .011″, tighten the knot with pliers or hemostats.
6. Adjust loop between fly hook and knot to desired size for specific fly performance. Trim excess tag.

This is a superb knot for tying bass flies to your leader. It's fast and simple to tie and is failproof; it has excellent wet-knot strength. It has three configuration options:

A small open-loop knot for maximum fly action and good balance;

A larger loop knot for slip shock absorption with heavy fish or rod strikes; and

Tight against the hook-eye to hold the leader hard against the fly. Unlike the clinch knot series, the Duncan loop tightened against a hook will not slip out or fail.

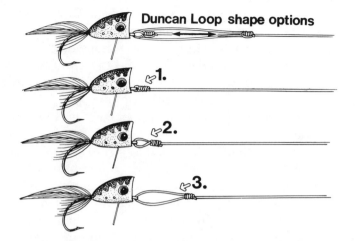

Duncan Loop shape options

Duncan Loop Options

When properly tightened, a wet Duncan Loop may be positioned to perform several options:

1. Cinched down tight next to fly—for leader control of fly's attitude.
2. Small open loop—to allow fly to move more independently of leader for more lifelike action, balance and floating, or sinking ability.
3. Large open loop—for shock absorption when leader is violently or excessively strained by fish, obstruction, or angler.

Before attaching your fly, practice tying the Duncan loop with some excess ten or twelve-pound-test nylon monofilament until you become efficient with it. Also practice forming various loop sizes. The tighter the Duncan loop knot is the less the loop will slip shut or close on the fly's eye. If properly tightened it will not slip closed during normal casting or retrieving but will be easy to open back with your fingernails if it slips closed on the strike or fight.

Practice all these recommended connections as many times as it takes for you to feel comfortable doing them quickly, neatly, and correctly. This investment will reward you with more fishing time and more success as you fish. Fly-line scraps or old fly lines make excellent, easy-to-see-and-handle practice materials. For this, you can cut eight or ten feet of fly line from the back of a weight-forward or level fly line without in any way hurting its practical length.

For practicing with nylon, use nylon of about ten to sixteen-pound-test or diameters of .010″ to .014″. These sizes are neither too stiff nor too soft to be hard to handle yet they wrap and tighten nicely and are easy to see while doing the knots.

Your backing should last for many years. The fly line will usually not need changing for at least two or three years of normal use and care. The leader, though, requires changing two or three times a season if you fish a lot. The tippet may need replacing several times a day and certainly each time you go fishing.

The fly needs to be replaced or retied regularly during a fishing day. The backing-to-fly-reel knot needs to be tied only once, backing-to-fly-line knot every two or three years, leader-to-fly-line knot three or four times a season, tippet knot two or three times a day, and the fly knot about one to ten times each fishing day. That's why practicing the surgeon's knot and the Duncan loop many times is important. All knots tend to weaken when they become wet or with use and age. Test all knots regularly and retie the tippet and fly-to-tippet knots regularly.

Wind or overhand leader knots. Wind or overhand leader knots are knots that you tie unintentionally as you cast. These simple overhand knots occur because of fishing accidents or casting faults. They are called wind knots because they're frequently caused when rushing or overpowering the casting stroke, trying to compensate for the wind's force against the cast. Wind knots most frequently occur on the tip or tippet section of the leader. Though nearly invisible, they weaken the leader's strength by as much as 50%! This is because the overhand knot continues to tighten on itself and cuts or squeezes itself when stressed. These knots must be removed. If the wind knot is not yet tight, it can simply be untied. If it *is* tight, you must cut the leader tip or tippet off to the wind knot and either retie the fly at that point or replace the section removed with a new piece of tippet material using the surgeon's knot and then retie the fly to the new tippet.

Wind knots occur less frequently on the heavier mid- or butt sections but if they do they may be untied or left there without severely weakening the leader. Check your leader frequently, especially on windy days or if you notice the leader or fly-line tip striking or tangling each other. In the casting section, I will discuss how to prevent wind knots from occurring.

Wind or Overhand Leader Knots

A knotless leader will be smooth if free of any tight wind knots.

1. A wind knot that has not tightened or weakened the leader yet can be removed by loosening and untying it.
2. A wind knot that has tightened and damaged the leader's strength cannot be untied. The leader must be replaced or repaired.

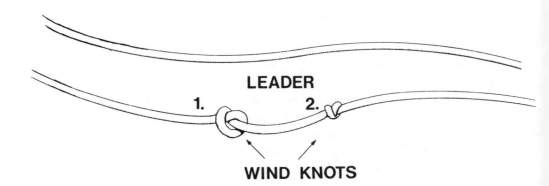

LEADER

1.   2.

WIND KNOTS

Droppers. There may be times when you wish to use two or more flies—called droppers—at one time. This is most commonly done simply by leaving a four to six-inch-long tag section on the leader-to-tippet surgeon's knot connection. Tie the dropper fly to the long tag with a Duncan loop or Trilene clinch knot.

Knot Tag and Dropper Fly

D1. Surgeon's Knot—When tying the Surgeon's Knot between leader tip and tippet, leave a long tag excess. Tie a dropper fly to the tag end with the Duncan Loop or Cinch Knot.
D2. Second Dropper Fly Option. Tie a section of tippet material to the hook bend using a closed Duncan Loop Knot. Trailer fly is tied to dropper end as shown, with a Duncan Loop.
D3. This arrangement can be removed or replaced easily by opening the Duncan Loop on the hook shank.

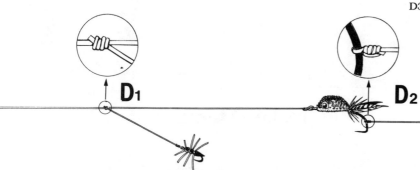

Bite or shock tippet. Bass do not have teeth, fins, or gill plates that can cut your leader to the fly; but many bass waters hold predator fish that do. To fish such waters without losing a lot of flies or to catch these other gamefish, you'll need to tie on a short tippet section of wire or extra-thick nylon monofilament that will resist being severed.

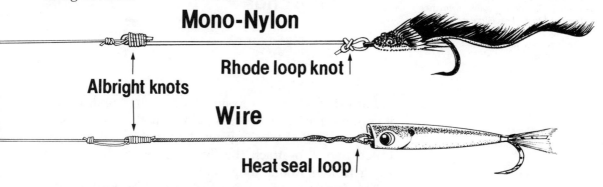

Monofilament and metal bite tippets.

For most of these bite-tippet sections, eighteen to thirty-pound-test nylon monofilament hardtype is ideal and preferred over the heavier and more-prone-to-kink wire tippets. Nylon bite tippets should be made from harder types of nylon.

The Albright knot is effective for this nylon-to-extra-heavy nylon or wire connection. Here are instructions for tying an improved slip-proof version of this popular knot.

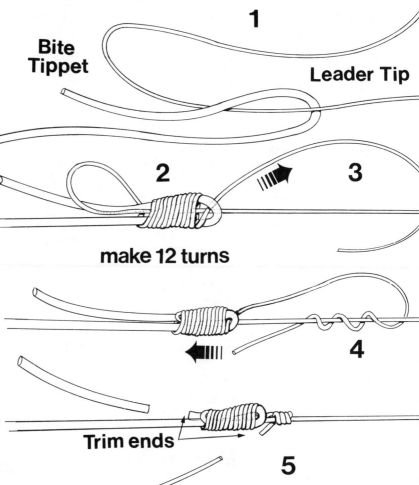

Improved Albright Knot

1. Form a short loop with bite tippet material and pass eight to ten inches of leader tip through side loop.
2. Grasp and close loop with fingers and wrap leader tip firmly and evenly around loop end twelve times. Pass leader tip through loop as shown.
3. Pull twelve wraps tight with leader's end.
4. Wrap leader's tip end around leader three times and pass tag end between first wrap, and pull wraps back tight against bite tippet loop.
5. Tug on both sides of knot to further tighten and test, then clip excess ends.

Note: If you are using a .012″ or larger leader tip you may need pliers to tighten the knot's wraps.

For fish that can cut braided wire coated with nylon, it is important and necessary. Attach the wire to the leader with the same improved Albright knot as illustrated here. To attach the fly to the nylon bite tippet use a Homer Rhode loop knot.

This knot provides a fixed open loop that allows the fly to move freely even though it is tied to thick, stiff material. Note, however, that this knot is *not* used with normal diameter tippets because it only has 50% knot strength.

To attach the fly to nylon-coated braided wire, simply pass the wire through the fly's eye, twist it four to six times around itself, and carefully heat the twists with a match flame or cigarette lighter until the nylon melts. Allow the wrap to cool and clip off the excess wire tag.

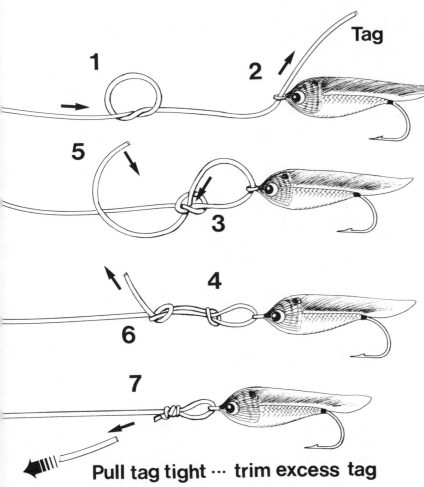

Pull tag tight ⋯ trim excess tag

Homer Rhode Loop Knot

1. Place a simple open overhand knot on leader bite tippet about three to six inches from its tag end.
2. Pass tag end through the eye of the hook.
3. Pass the tag end through the open overhand knot.
4. Snug the overhand knot down just in front of the hook eye as illustrated.
5. Take the tag end and pass it around leader to . . .
6. . . . form a second overhand snug knot.
7. Work the second knot back to the first overhand. With pliers, pull the knot very tight and trim excess tag off.

Note: You can also use this loop knot for soft braided wire tippet material if you tighten it correctly with pliers.

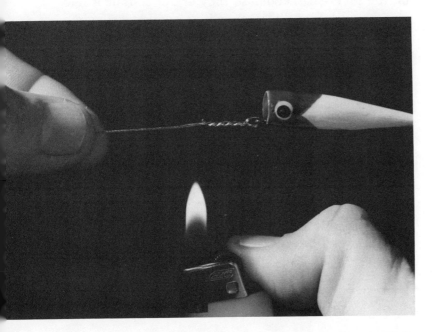

Nylon Coated Wire Fly Attachment

To attach a fly to a nylon-coated wire bite tippet, pass the wire through the hook's eye and make four to six twists around the wire with the tag end. Now, using a match or lighter flame, heat the twists until the nylon melts. Allow to cool and clip off the excess tag end with wire cutting pliers.

BITE TIPPET MATERIAL AND SIZE GUIDE (For species common to fresh and brackish bass waters)

Smaller sizes of material are for smaller fish or the small size should be changed after you've caught one or two larger fish.

Chain pickerel—twenty to thirty-pound monofilament

Northern pike—thirty to fifty-pound monofilament

Muskie—forty to sixty-pound monofilament or fifteen to twenty-pound-test braided wire

Gar—fifteen to twenty-five-pound braided wire

Bowfin (grindle or dogfish)—thirty to forty-pound monofilament or fifteen to twenty-pound braided wire

Snook—thirty to sixty-pound monofilament

Tarpon—thirty to eighty-pound monofilament or fifteen to thirty-pound braided wire

ASSEMBLY OF FLY TACKLE

Correct assembly of fly tackle for use can be simple and fast and will assure you of the best performance from your tackle.

Remove the fly rod from its protective tube and its cloth cover. Insert the rod's male ferrule into the female ferrule until resistance is felt. Align the guides on the different sections so they are in a straight line; you can adjust the alignment with a gentle twisting motion. Once the guides are aligned, apply a bit more push pressure to the ferrule to tighten the two pieces. Don't worry if the male ferrule seems a bit long; it is made this way to compensate for wear.

If the ferrules fit together loosely, take the rod apart and apply a thin film of beeswax or candle wax on the male ferrule; this will usually tighten up the fit without damage. If the ferrules feel gritty when you're putting them together, take them apart and clean them with soap and water. A cotton swab is excellent for cleaning inside the female ferrule.

Fly-reel attachment. Once the rod sections are together, attach the reel to the reel seat. Finger-tighten the screw-locking ring. Next, find the leader tip on the reel. Holding the rod handle, pull out the entire length

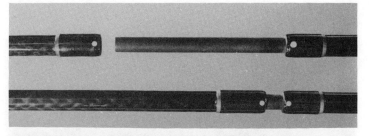

Fly-rod sections are joined by male and female ferrule parts. Line up dots and snugly fit sections together. Some gap is normal to compensate for wear.

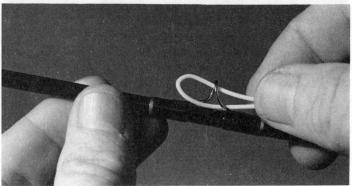

A double fly line is much easier to thread through guides than the leader's tip.

of leader and 1½ times the rod length of fly line. Now place the reel handle end of the rod on a clean, flat, nonabrasive surface (or have a companion hold it). If a clean surface is not available, place the rod handle and reel in your hat. Hold the rod near the ferrule and grasp the fly line two or three feet from the leader. Thread the doubled-over line through the guides toward the tip, taking care not to wrap the line around the rod between the guides. If possible, position or hold the fly rod with guides up to thread lines through. Pull the loose line and leader through the guides as you advance toward the tip. When you have passed two feet of the fly line through the tip-top, release it and give the rod a couple of quick casting motions. The loose line between the reel and tip will quickly clear the rod tip.

Leader straightening. The leader and fly line will have developed a coil set from being stored on the reel spool. This set must be straightened out for best performance. To do this, have someone hold the fly line or attach it to a door handle or another firm structure so that you can straighten the leader. Stroke the leader with your hand until you feel it warm up. Hold the leader straight and tight for a few seconds as it cools to reset the leader in a straight condition. Repeat until most of the coils or kinks are removed. Your bare hand is a much better leader-straightener than commercial leather or rubber straighteners. They tend to "burn" the leader.

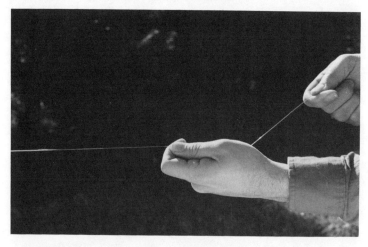

To straighten the leader efficiently, stretch it and hold taut, stroking it with the palm of your hand.

Fly-line straightening. A fly line without reel-spool memory coils will cast farther and more accurately than one with such coils. It will also float better and without slack, which improves strike detection and hook-setting.

Over a clean surface, pull thirty to fifty feet of fly line off the reel. Have someone hold one end or else attach it to a firm structure. Then pull the fly line tight until you feel it stretch just a bit. Hold it stretched for several seconds, release tension, and see if the line has straightened. If it hasn't, repeat this procedure or stretch and gently stroke the line surface. A fly line is particularly difficult to straighten when the air is below 45°. When air or water temperatures are near or below freezing, the fly line finish becomes hard. Under such conditions, the line cracks easily during stretching or fishing. To prevent cracking damage, avoid excessive stretching.

Fly to leader. Now you are ready to tie on the fly, using one of the knots previously recommended. If you are just going to practice casting, you can tie on a practice fly—one with neither a point nor barb.

When you assemble your tackle, be sure to place the empty cloth sack back in the fly-rod tube and put the lid back on the tube; this will assure that the cloth sack does not get wet or dirty and that neither it nor the lid get lost.

Fly-tackle disassembly. Proper disassembly of fly tackle is also important. It helps prevent damage and insures that the tackle will be ready the next time you need it.

When you stop fishing, reel in your line and make a few short, rapid false-casts to dry off the fly before removing it. Cut the fly off the tippet and place it in a hatband, on your fishing vest's fly patch, or in a well-ventilated fly box so it will dry completely.

To clear and dry your fly line, immediately or shortly after use lay it over the water or over a grit-free surface. With a clean cloth or paper towel in your rod hand, reel the fly line onto the reel spool while squeezing it with the towel. This removes most of the water and the dirty film a line acquires during fishing. Always make sure when you reel the fly line onto the reel that it spools on firmly and evenly. Guide it with your rod hand, using moderate tension. Too loose or uneven spooling may cause a bad tangle. If the fly line is wound on too tight, however, it may kink or set in small loops or curls.

Leader storage. As you wind the leader onto the fly reel, leave out about four to six inches of the tippet. This makes the fine tippet end much easier to find next time, and it also prevents the end from accidentally passing under the leader or line coils on the reel. If the leader slips under the coil of line on the reel, it's possible that a half-hitch will result, causing a tangle and/or loss of a large fish. Take the end of the leader and pass it out one of the reel-spool ventilation holes and back in another to keep it in place and prevent its getting lost in the spool.

Fly-reel storage. Remove the reel from the reel seat, wipe it clean, and dry it with a towel. If you have been fishing in brackish or saltwater, be sure to wash the salt deposits off the reel and fly line with fresh water. Wipe dry, then allow to air dry a few hours before storing. Place the reel in a well-ventilated bag or case to allow the damp fly line and backing and internal parts of the reel to dry.

Disassembling fly rod. Now disassemble the rod. If the ferrules seem stuck, have a companion help you separate them—both of you should hold onto a different section of the rod and then pull slowly. Wipe the rod clean and dry with a towel. Replace it in the cloth rod bag and protective case. Be sure not to get the inside of the rod case or the rod bag wet. When storing, leave the lid off the tube to make sure that the rod bag, inside of the rod tube, and the fly rod are completely dry. It is essential that the rod and cloth bag be dry.

Store your tackle in a dark, cool, dry area. Proper storage prevents damage and premature aging.

Always disassemble sections of your fly rod when storing it in a boat, car, or cabin, or when carrying it through dense foliage. Car doors, house doors, feet, and tree limbs are famous for their ability to break fly rods. Many more fly rods are broken as a result of carelessness than by fish and fishing.

4
Fly Casting for Bass

A clear understanding of fly-casting dynamics is your first major step toward becoming a good fly caster in the shortest time. Fly casting any type of fly for any gamefish works on the same dynamic principles. To become a good fly caster you will have to devote more time to practice and acquire more on-the-water experience than for the other casting methods, but your reward will be many times more satisfying. There is a poetic, hypnotic, almost sensuous sensation to casting a fly line and fly that seizes one's enthusiasm. A good fly caster seems artistically endowed as he or she scribes the fly line through graceful patterns.

To the casual observer or even spin and baitcasters, fly casting appears to be merely graceful waving of the fly rod and fly line back and forth through the air. But fly casting is a precisely timed and controlled cycle of stroking motions that energize and direct the fly line and fly in an accurate path to the water target.

First, remember that you are casting the fly line and that the leader and fly are pulled after it. When you cast, the fly line remains extended from the start to finish of the cast—no reel is used as in other casting methods.

The fly cast has four parts:

Pickup—lifting the extended fly line, leader, and fly up and off the water surface with the fly rod;

Up and back cast—stroking the fly rod up and back to propel the lifted fly line, leader, and fly up and behind you—to have the fly line in a straight position for the next part of the cast;

Forward down cast—stroking the fly rod forward and down to direct and deliver fly line, leader, and fly to the target area; and

Presentation—the settling of the fly, leader, and fly line to the target area.

After each cast is made and after the fly has been "fished" back, the same four-part casting technique is repeated.

Study the diagram to get a strong visual concept of these four parts. Note the following facts:

The length of the extended fly line remains more or less constant;

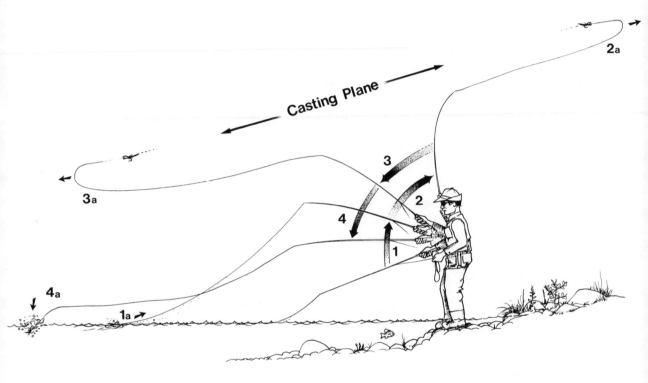

The Four Parts of a Fly Cast

1. Pick-up
1A. Start #2 when the leader and fly come off the surface
2. The up-and-back casting stroke
2A. Pause to allow the fly line, leader, and fly to unroll and straighten
3. The forward-and-down casting stroke
3A. Pause to allow the fly line, leader, and fly to unroll and straighten
4. Presentation
4A. Allow the fly, leader, and line to land on the water.

The paths the fly line travels back and forward are more or less straight, at a constant angle; this is called the "casting plane";

The directions the fly line travels are caused by the rod, hand, and arm stroke; and

As the fly line moves past the rod tip on the up and down strokes, a "loop" of fly line forms that rolls over on itself until the fly line, leader, and fly are fully extended.

All this control of arm/hand/fly rod and fly line occurs mainly because the heavy, relatively stiff fly line

must move *with and in the same direction* as the *tip* of
the *fly rod*. Precise control of the fly rod's movement
means precise control of the fly cast.

Two additional facts:

Loop control (loop shape and loop direction) is the
key to good fly casting. And the paths of the loops (the
casting plane) as they go back and forth is the key to fly-
casting efficiency and accuracy.

There are four general loop shapes common to fly
casting: *narrow, wide, open,* and *closed*.

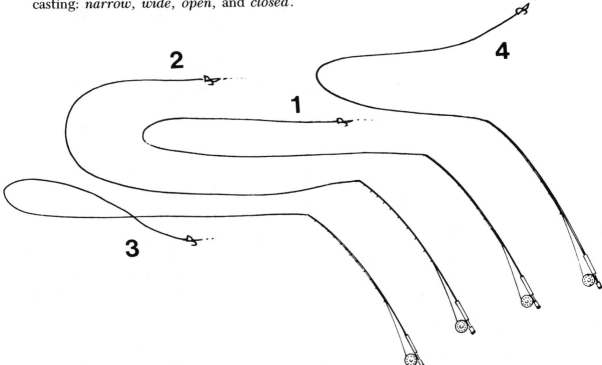

The Four General Loop Shapes

1. Narrow loop
2. Wide loop
3. Closed or tailing loop
4. Open loop

These four loops and their many variations are direct
results of the arc the rod tip is put through during the
power stroke. The moving rod tip forms or draws like a
pencil on paper the fly-line loop shape.

Which loop shape is correct? The narrow loop is the
most efficient for distance and best leader/fly delivery.
The wide loop has less efficiency because it will move
slower and have more wind resistance; but it may be
useful for some bass-fly presentations. The tailing and
open loops are loop deformities caused by poor casting
dynamics and are seldom if ever desireable.

The simplest way to understand and relate loop
shape and control to the fly rod and casting stroke is to
use the clock system.

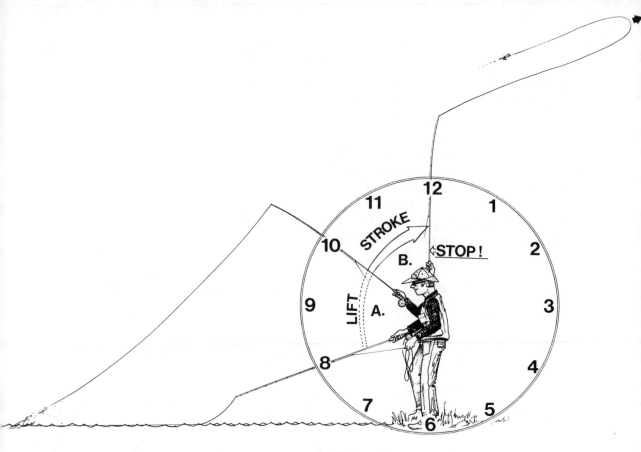

The Clock and the Fly Caster
RLS = Resultant loop shape and direction from the ten to twelve o'clock casting stroke

Study the diagram and visualize yourself standing with a large clock face at your side. The nine o'clock position is forward (the direction you are facing) and the twelve o'clock is directly above your head. The three o'clock position is behind you and the six o'clock position is at your feet. Now think of the fly rod as the clock hand.

To form a narrow loop, you might begin your cast with a pick-up motion from the water—eight o'clock lifting to ten o'clock.

For the up and backcast tight-loop power stroke, the rod should move from ten to twelve o'clock and stop there. The tight loop then forms, moving in the direction of the stroke up and in back of you and the stationary twelve o'clock rod tip.

Just as the line, leader, and fly straighten out above and behind you *(watch this movement)* you initiate your forward and down stroke for a tight loop. Do this by simply power-stroking from twelve o'clock to ten o'clock with the fly rod. *Stop the rod movement at ten o'clock!* Allow the tight loop to form and move forward and down toward the target area. It's that simple.

Now if you had stroked from ten to two or three o'clock (waved your rod through a larger arc) then from three back to ten o'clock, you would have two very wide, inefficient loops. The wide fly line and leader loop would not have taken your fly as far or as accurately as the narrow loop. Unfortunately, most beginning fly casters with the rod-waving concept, or those of you who have had experience with other casting methods, immediately fall into bad loop-shape habits—with nightmarish results. It's human nature if the wide loop is formed and the fly falls short to *increase* the rod arc and try to *force* the fly line to go out better. *Less* arc and *less* power are the solution!

The tailing loop is the most undesirable loop shape. It's caused when the caster either starts the forward stroke too soon (before the line can straighten out in back) or accelerates the cast too hard at first. In either case the rod tip (which is very flexible) dips sharply down or *shocks* with the overload of line weight and power causing a portion of the line moving with the stroke to do so also. This deformed, closed loop then catches itself near the end of the cast, causing tangles, wind knots, and poor presentations.

Remember that the movement of the rod tip forms the loop's shape. If the rod tip dips then straightens, that's what the fly line must do also. This dip deforms the loop shape.

The beginning fly fisher's commonest error is to *wave* the rod and create very wide or open loops; experienced spin and baitcasters will make the closed or tailing loop when first trying to fly cast. In addition, as fly fishers become better casters, they sometimes begin to force the rod for extra distance and develop tailing loops.

The degree of flex during the power stroke has a definite effect on loop shapes. Slow-action rods will consistently form wider loops and tailing loops than those with medium action. Medium-action rods will form loops a bit wider than those of fast-action rods. Medium-fast or fast-action fly rods are best for bass fly fishing because they will cast tighter, high-speed loops and are less likely to tip shock and form tailing loops.

BASIC FLY-CASTING PRACTICE PROCEDURE

Before beginning this section on fly-casting procedure be sure that you understand the section on fly-casting dynamics. It's best to begin your fly-casting practice under the direction of a qualified instructor—preferably *not* a spouse or fly-fishing friend (who might cause unnecessary emotional pressure). If friends want to help, make sure that first they read and understand this section on fly-casting theory and method so they will speak the same language and not confuse you. It's better for you to understand *this* text and go it alone than to accept the help of an unqualified instructor. Any skill as complex as fly casting may be accomplished in several ways. The right or best way *for you* may differ from another's. Be aware of this and don't get upset when you discover varying methods.

There are some fine video tapes on fly casting that will help you learn to cast; by all means view one or more of these before you start. (See the Bibliography for additional instructional materials.)

Choose for your practice an uncongested, calm, *nonflowing* water surface such as a pond, lake, or swimming pool. The area should also have an unrestricted space of at least forty feet behind you and twenty feet to either side. If such an area is not available, you might practice on a lawn or gymnasium floor. If you are casting over muddy, rough, or oily ground, spread out a groundcloth or canvas. This will protect your fly line from damage and dirt. Try to practice when there is little or no wind. If you cannot escape the wind, try to position yourself so that it blows from your left side if you cast with your right arm or vice versa.

It's important when practicing to use a practice fly of appropriate size and type. Without a fly, the tackle does not cast correctly and this will misdirect your learning responses. To avoid accidents, use a fly that has the hook point, barb, and bend removed; with a pair of pliers, cut the hook off at the bend. Another option is to tie about two inches of bright yarn or doubled pipe cleaner to the leader tip. Now straighten your leader and about forty feet of fly line as described in Chapter 3.

Hold the rod in your casting hand and then strip about thirty feet of line off the reel with your hand. Let this line fall to the ground at your feet. Grasp the fly and leader and pull about twenty-five feet of fly line out through the tip-top. Lay this line on the ground in a straight line behind you to its full length including the leader.

Three Hookless Practice Flies

Section of colorful yarn

Pipe cleaner

Bass fly with hook clipped off

Facing the direction in which you intend to cast, place your feet about 1½ feet apart and move your casting-arm foot a bit behind the other. If you are casting over water, stand about three or four feet from the edge; be sure the area is clean so that excess line does not tangle or become dirty. By positioning your feet as recommended you will be standing slightly sideways of the direction in which you intend to cast. This stance is necessary to allow you to watch both your forward and backcast unroll. *You cannot learn to fly cast well if you do not observe both your forward and backward casts.*

Hold the rod, reel, and line as shown in the accompanying illustration.

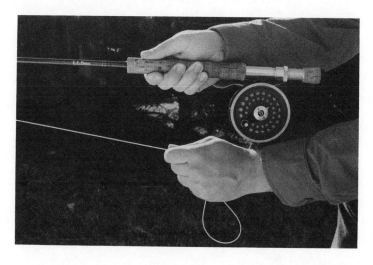

Correct grip on fly-rod handle and fly line while practicing fly casting.

Make sure that your thumb is on top of the rod handle and that you have positioned your grip on the handle comfortably. Avoid placing your index finger on the top of the handle, for this position will not give you the stability you need. Avoid placing your thumb on the side of the handle, too—this splits your control. You do not want the rod to twist or rotate in your grip. Hold the fly line between the reel and the first stripping guide with your other hand to maintain line control.

The hand used to hold the fly line while you cast and fish should be thought of as your reel. It performs many fly and fly-line control functions. But at first simply teach that hand to hold the line tightly at the rod. If you release it as you practice cast, you will create problems.

Before you start to cast, take a few slow, deep

breaths and relax. With the fly rod in about the one o'clock position, cast forward, putting the fly in front of you in the water or grass. Now begin to make the four parts of a fly cast—Pick-up, Up and back cast, Forward and down cast, and Presentation.

To make a perfect basic fly cast, each of these four steps must be accomplished correctly. It's natural for you to emphasize the forward and down cast most, and the pick-up least. But the single *most important* part of the cast *is* the *pick-up.* It is the foundation of every cast. If this is not correct, it is impossible to proceed with a perfect cast. Here are the relative values of each part of the cast:

1. Pickup—30%   3. Forward and down cast—15%
2. Up and backcast—25%   4. Presentation—10%

In our years at the L.L. Bean Fly Fishing School, we have proved that practically *every* bad casting habit or problem can be directly traced to an incorrect pickup.

Pick-up. With the rod tip straight forward and almost touching the water or ground (about eight o'clock) begin to lift in a deliberate accelerating motion, raising your arm or picking up the fly line resting on the water surface. This pick-up motion should be slightly off the side of your casting shoulder and upward. Keep your *wrist straight (locked)* to avoid any fly-rod tip rotation as you lift with the rod and arm; resist the tendency to "rip" the fly line off the water with a nervous jerk. When all but the leader and fly are off the water, the

Correct Pick-Up Method to Begin Cast

1A. Begin pick-up with rod tip almost touching the water surface and pointing toward the fly.
1B. With the fly-line hand, pull any slack out of the fly line between your hand and the fly.
2. Immediately after Step 1B, begin to pick your fly line up off the water with a smooth, steady rod-lifting motion. Try to use your height and arm length to raise the line up into the casting plane rather than rotating the fly rod to a high angle. *Study this diagram carefully.*
3. Watch your fly-line tip/leader/fly area and try to pick up the line to at least this point; then, *without pausing,* allow the fly to leave the water smoothly so that the line and rod angle are in the best casting-plane position.

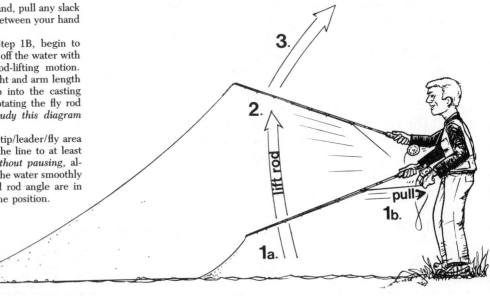

rod angle should be somewhere between ten and eleven o'clock. Your line hand and arm should be held slightly forward and low and kept relaxed at your side through all four parts. *Do not bring it up across your chest and back with your casting arm.*

Up and backcast. Without any pause after the pickup, begin a direct rod and arm stroke up and back, with a gradual accelerating motion or power application—with the energy needed, say, to toss a golf ball that high and far behind you. Ideally, moving the tip from ten o'clock to twelve o'clock—but *no farther* than one o'clock—before stopping the stroke is best. You're trying to throw the fly line and fly up and over yourself from off the water so that it will straighten out above and behind you. *You must watch the fly line to do so!* This way you can see whether you have stopped at the right clock position and whether you have given the stroke enough power; you will then know precisely when to start the third phase, which is just before the leader and fly come straight back and begin to fall.

If you stand correctly, you can watch your backcast. This is an absolute must if you want to develop a correct and well-timed up-and-back cast and a precisely timed forward-and-down cast stroke.

Forward and down cast. With your fly-rod tip at about one or twelve o'clock and watching the fly line straighten out above and behind you, begin a slow accelerating forward and down stroke. Do this mostly with your forearm (twelve to ten o'clock) and use it and your wrist's power at the last and maximum power point (eleven to ten o'clock). Stop the rod motion, *keeping the tip high at ten o'clock*, and watch the fly-line loop form and move forward past the rod and toward the water and/ground.

Presentation. As the fly line, leader, and fly reach the extent of their length forward, begin to follow the falling line down to nine or eight o'clock with your fly-rod tip until the fly line and fly rest on the water's surface.

Repeat this four-part procedure for three to five minutes to get the feel of your tackle and casting. Stay relaxed and loose; don't hold your breath or rush the casting cycles. If your back or forward casts are weak or falling short, increase your stroke power. Remember overcoming the water's hold on the fly and fighting gravity takes more power than casting that same load "downhill" *with* gravity. Most beginning fly casters reverse these power needs, which is incorrect. Work *very* hard to keep the ten to twelve or one o'clock arc in your back and forward casting to assure a good loop shape and *correct casting plane*.

The overhead or overshoulder casting position is the best to begin with since it relates easily to the clock method. But as soon as you have a clear understanding of the clock and of loop shapes and casting planes, it's easier to practice casting with a half *sidearm* position. This is because your arm and shoulder are more comfortable and familiar with making sideways strokes— with baseball bats, tennis rackets, and the like. Also, sidearmed, your fly line will travel a bit lower and more to the side, making it easier to watch your backcast and rod-tip positions than when casting overhead.

When you actually fly cast for bass, you will use some form of sidearm casting position for most of your casts. The lower-angle cast is also less hazardous, less affected by wind, and less visible to fish. But never forget the clock angle; think now that the clock face has been tilted over at the same plane the fly rod moves through at your side.

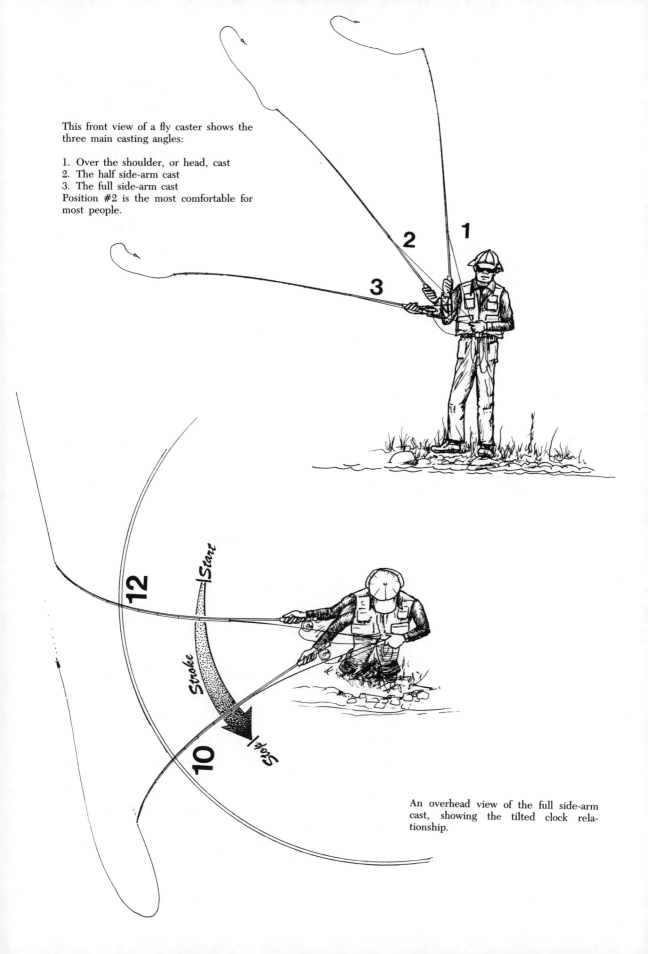

This front view of a fly caster shows the three main casting angles:

1. Over the shoulder, or head, cast
2. The half side-arm cast
3. The full side-arm cast

Position #2 is the most comfortable for most people.

An overhead view of the full side-arm cast, showing the tilted clock relationship.

As you get some feel for casting, let's add further suggestions. Place a hula hoop or dish pan on the surface, to serve as a target. Look at this target as you begin each forward and down stroke, and make that stroke toward the target. It's not necessary to hit the target but this object will motivate you and develop

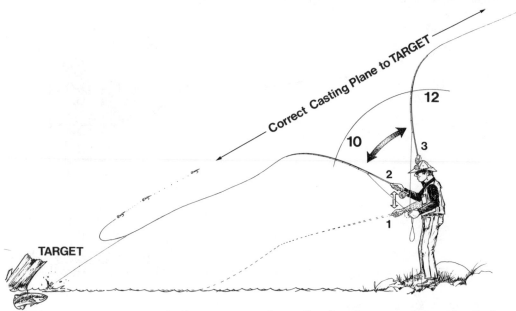

To hit the target area with your fly, adjust the casting plane so that the fly travels in a more or less straight path to the target. Note in this diagram that just as the fly turns over the leader it strikes the target area.

1. Pick-up begins at seven or eight o'clock to about nine-thirty o'clock—to the casting-plane angle needed to hit the target.
2. Up-and-back stroke from nine-thirty o'clock to eleven-thirty o'clock, so that the fly and line travel in that correct plane.
3. The forward-and-down stroke from eleven-thirty o'clock to nine-thirty o'clock puts the fly on target. Now lower your rod back to the first position in order to fish the fly.

your eye. Adjust your casting plane so that the loop's direction travels straight toward the target, so that the fly strikes the target area just as it turns over the leader. Most bass-fly presentations will require the fly to strike the target area, not fall on it from above.

If the fly and the fly line strike the water in a splashy pile short of the target, you're most likely bringing the rod tip too far down, perhaps to nine or eight o'clock, before the fly line can extend to the target. Remember again—*the fly line always follows the direction of the tip*. In this cast, you are forcing it down with a low rod tip, killing the presentation.

If your fly line and fly go out high over the target, then fall back to your side of the target in a messy heap of fly, leader, and fly-line tip, this is because your down and forward rod stroke is too high ("high stroking" the presentation). This causes the fly line, leader, and fly to straighten out at a high angle; then the leader and fly are pulled back toward the rod tip by the falling line's weight. Most likely this "high stroking" is caused by your allowing your rod tip and backcast to go too far back and down to the two, three, or four o'clock position. This causes a change in the correct plane from ten/twelve/ten to ten/two/twelve. This is the most common fly-casting error.

When you've learned the four parts of the cast, it's time to try some false casting.

False casting is merely eliminating the presentation and pick-up sequences for one or more casts while repeating the up-and-back and forward-and-down parts continuously. False casting is used to extend fly-line length, to hold the fly in the air above the water until you pick a target, or to remove water from a soggy, floating fly. *Most bass fishing requires limited false casting!* To false cast, eliminate the presentation and as the line straightens forward above the water start another up-and-back cast. Don't let the fly hit the water but in a back-and-forth casting cycle hold the fly up in the air. At first, practice doing one false cast; then do two or three. False casting can be tiring so don't overpractice until your arm has built up some endurance.

As you practice resist the temptation to extend the fly-line length. Stay with about twenty-five or thirty feet or a length you feel comfortable using. Having a fixed-distance target will help you avoid the temptation to use too much line. Too much line will cause timing, loop, casting plane, and presentation problems, and this will discourage you. Most bass fly-rodding I do averages about thirty to forty feet; longer distances are seldom required and are not as productive. In time, however, if you have correct technique you will be able to achieve longer casting distances with ease. Good fly casting is not based on strength but on timing and technique. Expert fly casters appear to make long casts effortlessly. This is because they do not throw the fly line with their arm speed but correctly load or energize the fly rod and then allow it to unflex and *cast* the fly line almost as a bow casts an arrow. The fly rod is a fine casting tool that gives you so much leverage you need only a small amount of strength to fly cast. That's why you can fish effectively for bass from age nine to age ninety.

ROLL CASTING

Roll casting is a second major cast that you should learn. It uses the same fly-casting dynamics and like the false cast merely modifies the basic four-part cast. What is a roll cast?　　It's a basic overwater fly cast without the backcast step.

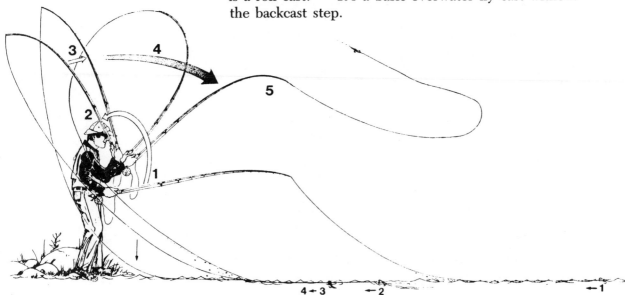

Basic Steps of the Roll Cast

1. Pick-up. Begin with your rod forward and tip next to the water—a slow-motion rod lift to about nine o'clock. The line and fly will move toward you on the water. Now with the same slow motion begin to elevate your arm and rod by moving the tip up and back to the two o'clock position with your rod in a high half side-arm position. The white arrow highlights this move. The fly and the end of the fly line continue to move on the water surface toward you.
2. Pause to allow the fly line to reach a perpendicular from the rod's tip. This positions the main portion of the fly-line weight just behind you.
3. Now raise your arm a bit more and move your rod back to the one o'clock position, as shown by the arrow. Note that the fly is closer, but still on the water.
4. Forward-and-down stroke. *Without pause* from Step 3, begin a *smooth, gradual, accelerating* stroke from twelve-thirty o'clock to ten o'clock toward the target area just as you would with a regular forward-and-down stroke.
5. Stop the forward-and-down stroke and note how a line loop will form and move in the direction of the target. The fly line behind you and on the water will be propelled up and forward with the force of the stroke, pulling the fly with it. *Do not allow the rod tip to drop* to more than the ten o'clock position until the line loop and fly are well on their way to the target.

DIAGRAM OF A ROLL CAST

The roll cast must be practiced over water, never dry surfaces. This is how it's done:

Pickup (most important part). With the fly line extended forward on the water and your rod tip pointed low and toward the fly line, begin a slow arm and rod-lifting motion that ends with your arm extended up and to the side with the rod tip pointing at two o'clock. Now pause a second or two. This pickup motion should slide the fly line, leader, and fly on the water toward and slightly to your side (the half sidearm rod position). Do this pickup motion in slow motion. The fly line you have lifted off the water will sag down with the pause to the two o'clock position beside and behind your shoulder.

Forward and down cast. After the pause, move your fly rod to the one or twelve o'clock position. From there begin the same basic forward-and-down casting power stroke toward the target. Stop the tip at ten o'clock. There is a temptation at this point to lower or stroke the tip down too far, even striking the water with it. *Do not* let this happen or the fly line, leader, and fly will simply pile up on the water somewhere between the rod tip and target. You need to make a basic forward cast so the fly-line loop will form and move forward with leader and fly.

Presentation. As the loop unrolls, the leader and fly follow it as the line falls to the water; follow the loop with the rod tip. That is a completed roll cast.

Repeat this procedure a number of times. Don't rush the pick-up. Don't accelerate the forward-and-down cast too abruptly and make the rod tip arc go only from twelve to ten o'clock. Practice the roll cast in the side-arm and back-hand casting positions when you've got the knack of the half sidearm position. This casts works without a backcast because you place enough fly-line weight behind you with the two o'clock rod angle pickup and pause to pull the remaining line and fly up and forward off the water as the forward-moving loop passes over them.

The roll cast has almost unlimited use for bass fly fishing. Here are some of its most important uses:

When an obstacle is above or behind you, you can still make a forward cast without hanging your fly on the obstacle;

It's a perfect method for picking up or straightening slack fly line;

A modified roll cast allows you to swim a bass fly in any direction on the water;

To make lifting and pick-up of a sink-tip or sinking fly line from the water easy;

To unhook your fly when snagged on an obstacle;

To make a slow, delicate fly presentation;

To assist in hook setting when excess fly-line slack is unavoidable; and

For repositioning your fly line if it should blow or drift too far to your side for safe or correct pick-up.

THE FLY-LINE HAND

As you hold the fly rod to cast, fish, hook, and fight bass, your other hand is in constant use, too. It must hold the fly line, control its slack or tension, give fly line out, assist in casting, pull line in, assist in striking, and pull the fish in manually or with the fly reel.

Let's add this hand into consideration as you practice casting. A bass fly fisher uses the fly-line hand on each cast to tighten the fly line on pickup, to extend more fly line as he casts for extra distance, and then to retrieve and animate the fly. If the bass strikes, the fly-line hand helps set the hook, control the line and fly-reel operation throughout the battle, then with net or bare hand land the fish. Clearly the fly-line hand has a key role in fly fishing.

Before you begin your pick-up, when the fly-rod tip is at its lowest angle, use your line hand to pull out straight and tight any slack you caused before or as your lowered the rod tip for the pick-up start. This simple tightening of the fly line will assure you a much more efficient pick-up.

As you lift the line off the water, hold the fly line tightly in your line-hand fingers, keeping your line hand and arm stationary; or better, you can make a short downward pull or "haul" with it. This simple technique will increase the fly-line speed, which helps it move off the water and upward. This improves pick-up efficiency.

Using the fly-line hand for extra distance. If you want to cast farther, add extra power to the forward-and-down casting stroke. Then as the over-accelerated fly line and fly move well forward of the rod tip, you should feel a slight line tug on your fly-line hand as a result of this extra line speed. As this occurs, loosen your finger hold on the fly line and the extended line that is tugging will pull out more line from your hand proportional to its excess energy. This is called "shooting line." The fly-line hand must be trained to feel or sense this pull and release the fly line precisely for maximum effect. When you first try this your anxiety becomes excessive and you will probably release the fly line *during the power stroke*, which will give slack and spoil the cast. This mistake actually *reduces* your distance. Delay the line release; watch the line move forward until you *feel* the tug. Be careful that with the extra power you add you still accelerate slowly and maintain the rod-tip stop position between eleven and ten o'clock. If the rod goes lower on the stroke, you'll force the fly line to dive steeply at the water rather than *unroll* over it; this kills or shortens rather than lengthening the cast. Remember to watch the fly line move well forward; as it does, if you've given the cast enough extra power, you'll feel the fly line tug and release properly for the "shoot."

Establishing absolute fly-line hand control. As your fly nears the water, you should have fly-line and rod control over it. This is done by establishing a two-point (two-hand) hold on the fly line. This allows you to control precisely the tension on the fly-line system for animating the fly, retrieving it, detecting strikes, hooking bass, and manually pulling the fish to you. *This is an absolute must for successful bass fly fishing.*

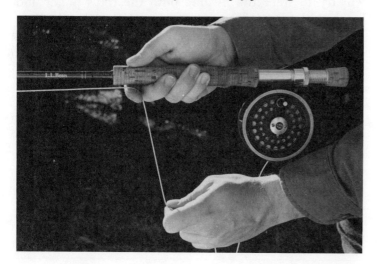

The correct hand and line position for two-point control. Note that the fly line is gripped under the index finger of your rod hand and held with the fingers of your reel-line hand.

The two-point control method is accomplished like this:

1. As the fly line, leader, and fly begin to fall to the surface, begin to move your fly-line hand toward your extended rod hand. Keep your eyes on the fly.

2. Extend down the first or index finger of your rod hand from its grip on the fly-rod handle.

3. With your fly-line hand's fingers, make direct contact with your rod hand's extended finger, placing the fly line across the extended finger. Grasp the line with the rod's index finger and press it against the handle of your rod. Do not release your fly-line hand's grip on the fly line. Now you are controlling the fly line in a two-handed hold.

4. With this two-point method, you have the best possible control on the fly line and fly for controlling initial slack and tension, for animating and retrieving the fly, for setting the hook on a strike, and for controlling slack and tension on the fly line as the bass fights.

If you have spin-fished, an excellent way to understand this two-point control system is to consider the rod-hand index finger's grip on the fly line as the bail of a spinning reel and the fly-line hand grip as the spinning-reel handle. If you fail to close the bail or engage the handle you have no line and lure control. That is what happens when you do not use fly fishing's two-point system.

5. Release of two-point control. As you begin the pick-up for the next cast, release the rod-hand's finger hold on the fly line.

As you practice this two-point control technique, you will try to steer the fly line onto the rod's finger and reach with the rod hand and fly rod for the fly line. Both are incorrect. If you do either, you will encounter delays or problems. Remember that the *fly-line hand* must move to the rod finger. Reach and put the fly line right onto the rod hand's index finger.

Each time you cast and present the fly, establish two-point control. Retrieve the fly by making a few short line strips with your line hand. Relax your rod-finger grip each time you pull on the line with your line hand. Then as you reach for additional lengths of line just behind your rod finger, tighten your rod-finger grip so you will not allow the fly line to be slack or loose. Do not reach for more fly line above or in front of the rod hand, *always behind the hand*.

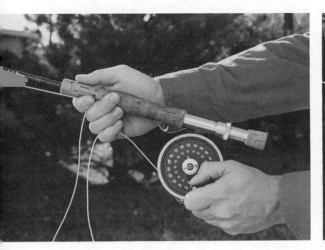

Practice this with every cast from this point on until it is automatic to do so; this is something you *must* do each time you fish a bass fly.

Here are two other line-hand functions to clear up any confusion or questions about retrieving that you might have.

You can use two-point control to fight a small fish but it is always best to eliminate the excess fly line you pull in that coils down loosely between your hand and the fly reel. To solve this potential tangling problem, hand the slack line to your rod hand's small finger and begin to wind the slack fly line onto the reel; use your small rod-hand finger to provide tension and level-winding control to the spooling fly line.

Once all this slack is on the fly reel, release both rod-finger grips on the line. Now control the retrieving or giving of fly line during the fight with the reel handle. Use the cranking speed and your fly rod to control slack and fight tension until the fish tires and is landed. This reeling is the same as you would use to fight a fish with other reel methods.

It may be obvious but if not: most of the fly's movements on the water are done by fly-line hand pulls and the movement of the fly-rod tip. As you make these pulls, you are shortening the amount of fly line you have extended. Try at this point to keep at least twenty feet of line extended for casting weight to initiate the next cast. Then as you make the next cast and want to extend the fly line and fly out farther, do so by overpowering and shooting extra fly line out as explained earlier. As you practice, try to work on each of these procedures.

(Left) The correct way to reel up slack line between the rod handle and the reel without losing tension on the line, fly, or hooked fish.

(Right) The correct rod and reel-hand positions for fighting a fish directly from the reel.

TYPES OF FLY CASTS

Besides the two basic fly casts, there are variations you will want to master to take full advantage of the potential of fly fishing for bass.

Sidearm cast. For this variation of the basic four-part or roll cast, hold the rod to your side so that the line travels lower and the loop lies on its side. This allows you to keep the line low and out of the fish's sight, under wind, or to cast under obstacles.

Backhand cast. This is simply an opposite sidearm cast. The rod and casting arm are placed across your body so that the line and fly are cast to that side. This gives you the advantage of the sidearm cast with another cast angle.

Underhand cast. A basic sidearm cast but done with an underhand casting stroke so fly line and fly travel very low or skip over the water. This is an excellent way to present a bass fly very delicately.

Skip cast. A sidearm cast delivered with extra-fast speed and low angle so that the fly hits the water and skips to the target. This is a great technique for casting a fly far back under low overhanging obstructions.

Curve cast. A cast that causes the fly and leader to curve right or left as they land. This cast is helpful for casting behind obstacles or to prevent fish from seeing the line over them before they see the fly.

Shooting line. Shooting line is similar in purpose to working out line. It is accomplished in either the backward or forward cast by using considerably more power than is needed to cast the line already extended. In either the backward or forward cast, slack line is fed out just as the moving loop reaches its end, thus pulling or shooting the extra slack out with it. Shooting line out reduces the number of false casts needed and aids distance casting.

Hauling. This is a technique for increasing line speed or overall fly-casting efficiency by using the power of both the rod arm and the free hand arm. The caster, just as the power stroke is applied with the fly rod, simultaneously pulls down on the taut fly line below the first stripper guide. This pull, or haul, increases the line's forward or backward speed.

Double-hauling involves hauling on both the forward and backward strokes. Hauling should not be attempted until you have mastered loop control. Only then does it become a useful method for better line pick-up and for making long, powerful casts. Hauling *before* you have mastered loop control will have an adverse effect on your overall casting ability.

Mending. Mending line is a technique of repositioning the fly line and leader on moving water (wind-blown surface or flowing water). It is accomplished by using various rod-lifting and roll-casting movements. When you are fishing streams, mending line can be as important as casting.

5
Bass Flies

Bass will eat or attack a wider range of live creatures than any other fish. No other artificials can imitate these creatures as well as flies do. To take fullest advantage of the possibilities fly fishing offers you to catch bass in all types of water year round, you should know what fly designs are available, what they do, and when to use them.

Six bass fly types cover most of the potential:

Dry flies are specifically designed to sit and float on the water's surface. Mostly they imitate various terrestrial and adult aquatic insects. The dry fly floats because it is made with a light wire hook, hair, or feather fibers and synthetics that are light weight and are waterproofed to remain dry. These materials cling to the surface tension of the water.

Dragon fly

Damsel fly

Moth bug, or Hair Gerbubble Bug

Three fluttering floating flies that are deadly when bass are leaping out of the water to catch such large insects as dragon flies, moths, and damsel flies. These flies parachute slowly to the water, like live insects, giving the bass a chance to catch them above the water or exactly when they land.

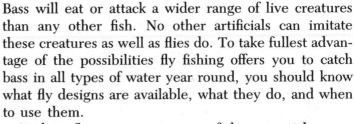
Tail   Body   Wing   Head   Hackle

A bass dry fly, with parts labeled.

Dry flies that imitate ants, beetles, grasshoppers, wasps, spiders, moths, crane flies, caddisflies, stoneflies, damsel flies, and dobson flies can be effective in streams and lakes for bass. The larger sizes—size 12 to 2 (½″ to 3″) are usually most attractive to bass.

Use dry flies when you notice fish making frequent splashes or see insects fluttering above or resting or struggling on the water's surface. Try to select a fly similar in size, shape, and color to the naturals you see and give the fly the same movement as the insects you have observed. Dry-fly fishing for bass and other cool or warmwater fish is usually most productive in late spring, summer, and early fall when water temperatures are 60° to 80°F.

Surface flies Bass Bugs or topwater bugs are designed to float more or less in the surface swimming position. These "topwater" bugs are the most popular of all bass flies, especially when the water temperature runs from 60° to 80°F. Bass love to attack struggling creatures on the surface and these surface flies draw vicious strikes. This is because they represent all sorts of "bugs" bass love, such as adult dragonflies, grasshoppers, moths, locusts, larger beetles, as well as noninsects such as small birds, frogs, minnows, snakes, bats, turtles, and mice.

There are two basic types of surface flies—hard and soft-bodied. The heads and/or bodies of these flies are made with buoyant material. The hard-head bug is usually made of rigid cork, balsa wood, cedar, or plastic. The soft bug has a head and/or body of deer hair, elk hair, antelope hair, or sponge rubber. Both types are popular but the hard head is more effective when the action is fast and the soft type better for slower action or when closer imitation of naturals is required.

Bass will usually hold onto the soft-bodied bug several times longer than the hard body because these feel or taste more realistic to them. This is important if the bug is sitting still or moving slowly, because setting the hook takes more time than when you're using a taut line and a fast-moving bug. If your reaction is slow, soft bodies help a lot.

Head and body designs vary according to what type of swimming action and noise is required to simulate the food creature.

The *Popper* design has a blunt or cupped face that when twitched or jerked makes a splashy, popping, or gurgling disturbance; bass are strongly attracted to the sights and sounds of such flies. With some practice you can make a good bass popper "talk" to the fish. This

Six Productive Dry Flies

Group 1 Aquatic Insects

Mayfly

Caddis fly

Stone fly

Group 2 Terrestrial Insects

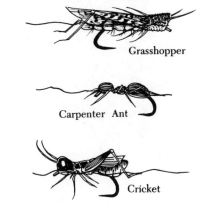

Grasshopper

Carpenter Ant

Cricket

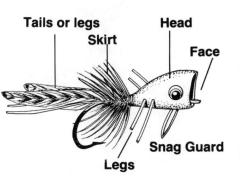

Tails or legs   **Head**
Skirt   **Face**
Snag Guard
Legs

Parts of a surface bass bug.

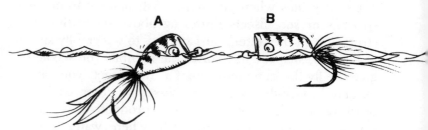

Surface bass flies are generally more effective if they hang down from the surface like Bug A. Bug B is too parallel. The hook point should be placed well behind and below the bug's body (Bug A) for best hooking.

Six Surface Fly Types
Hard body

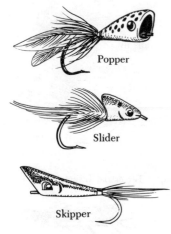

Popper

Slider

Skipper

Soft Body

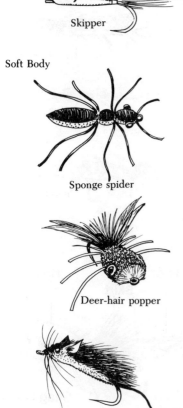

Sponge spider

Deer-hair popper

Deer-hair Mouse (slider)

talking would be sounds a struggling creature would make or those of another small fish splashing or feeding at the surface. These high-frequency sounds alert and direct bass to them. Poppers are a lot of fun to fish because of this action and the way bass break the surface to suck them down or come leaping out violently on top of the popper.

The *slider or waker* has a bullet-shaped nose and head that when twitched or pulled makes a wake and a low-frequency sound as it slides through the surface film. Sliders imitate calmer surface-swimming minnows, mice, water snakes, and the like. Bass are sometimes cautious because of clear water or calm surfaces; at such times sliders often outfish poppers because they make less disturbance and noise.

The *skipper bug* has an angled head that causes it to plane up, across, and over the water's surface when rapidly retrieved like a minnow that is leaping out of the water to escape a predator's attack. Skippers mostly imitate open-water school baitfish such as shad, shiners, and smelt that are being chased by such predators as bass, stripers, and snook.

Most soft-bodied floating flies made from deer, elk, or antelope hair will float without waterproofing. Usually, however, it's best to waterproof the hair body because this prevents the hair from absorbing water weight. A lighter bug will cast easier and swim on the surface better. Rub a small amount of a paste silicon compound such as Dave's Bug Flote or Gink into the body hair (not the legs or tails). Do this each time before you use the hairbug and sometimes when you are fishing it and the bug gets heavy or will not swim and pop as it should.

Floating diver. The "diver" fly like the floating fly has built-in buoyancy, but also a head design that

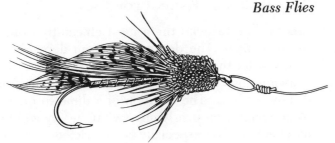

Muddler Minnow—one of the most versatile and effective bass flies. It can be dressed to float, dive, or swim, and looks like many bass foods.

causes it to plane or dive beneath the surface if you make a steady pull on the floating fly line and leader. The dive will cease when the pull is stopped and the diver will rise or float back to the surface. Such bass flies can accurately and effectively imitate the natural actions of such aquatic foods as frogs, salamanders, water snakes, turtles, injured or surface-feeding minnows, and diving insects. The clever bass fly-rodder can imitate all these once he's mastered fly action and retrieving techniques. At times bass are attracted to and excited by surface disturbance but will not readily hit at the surface. At such times the diver is the answer. This is particularly true early and late in the season when water temperatures are just a bit too cool for active top-water feeding (55° to 65°F.).

Swimming flies are made to sink below the surface at various rates according to what they imitate and where or how deep the bass are located. This large group of effective bass flies are commonly called wet flies, streamers, bucktails, leeches, and similar names by trout fly fishers. They imitate an enormous range of bass foods, including minnows, leeches, aquatic insect nymphs, shrimp, crabs, eels, lampreys, and salamanders.

Swimming flies, because they are usually out of sight, require more patience to fish properly; they are not as popular as surface flies and surface divers. But they are just as effective or more so, especially when water temperatures are from 55° to 75°F. Through the later winter, spring, and late fall months they are much more effective than surface flies in most bass waters. Also, all fish prefer to feed beneath the surface if they have their choice, for this is easier and less hazardous.

Most swimming flies sink slowly. The floating fly line is ideal for fishing them one to four feet deep, but use a

Two Types of Surface-Diving Bass Flies

Deer-Hair Head Diver

Billed Wiggling Diver

Three Effective Deer-Hair Head Divers

Frog

Crippled Minnow

Water Snake

sink-tip line to swim them most efficiently from five to ten feet deep. The depth they swim depends on how long you let them sink and how fast you retrieve them.

Swimming fly-and-spinner combinations can be deadly for bass. The addition of a dime to quarter-size blade spinner on nearly any swimming fly will increase its effectiveness, especially in restricted-vision waters. The flash and noise of the spinners help bass find the fly faster.

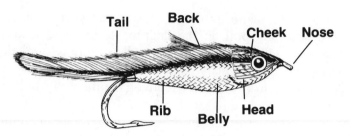

Seven Swimming Flies

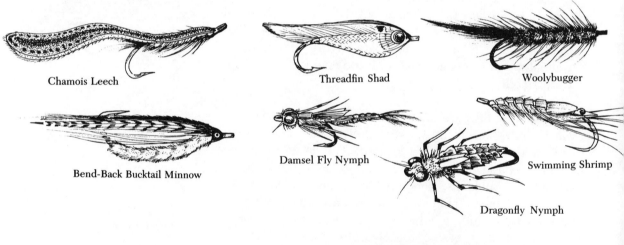

Chamois Leech

Threadfin Shad

Woolybugger

Bend-Back Bucktail Minnow

Damsel Fly Nymph

Swimming Shrimp

Dragonfly Nymph

Two Popular Spinner-and-Fly Combinations

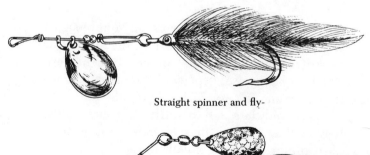

Straight spinner and fly-

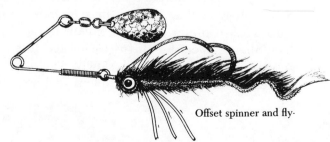

Offset spinner and fly-

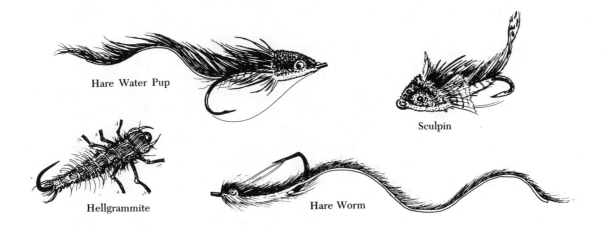

Hare Water Pup

Sculpin

Hellgrammite

Hare Worm

Bottom flies must sink rapidly to the bottom, so they are usually made with water-absorbent materials on a heavy hook with lead-wire weighting. These flies imitate various bottom-living or bottom-foraging creatures bass eat or are angered by, such as sculpin minnows, suckers, darters, minnows, aquatic insect nymphs, bullhead catfish, salamanders (water dogs or mud puppies), and similar creatures.

Bottom flies are not popular with many bass fly fishers but they are with bass. They are effective year-round when fished where bass live. Sink-tip and full-sinking fly lines with short leaders are best for keeping the bottom flies next to the bottom as you fish them.

The jig fly is similar to the bottom fly except that it has most of its extra sinking weight placed in the fly's head; this makes it sink vertically and sit on the bottom, nose first and tail up. This jigging design creates a hopping or jumping action off the bottom or in open water that bass go crazy for.

Bottom Crawling Flies

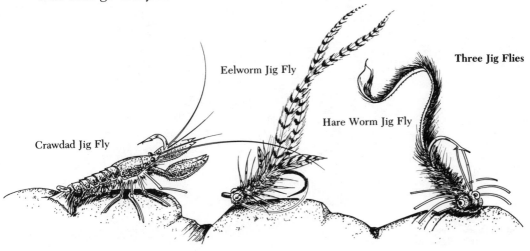

Eelworm Jig Fly

Hare Worm Jig Fly

Three Jig Flies

Crawdad Jig Fly

To "jig" the fly you must use a floating or slow-sinking line so that you can pull the fly upward with each pull or jerk. Then allow the fly slack to dive down again for the next hop or "jig." Some natural bass foods such as crayfish and sculpin have this sort of swimming pattern but bass will hit almost any fly pattern or imitation if it is jigged near them.

GOOD BASS FLY PROPERTIES

These six groups of bass flies in sizes ranging from one-half inch to eight inches long or hook sizes of 12 to 5/0 with all sorts of water actions, shapes, and colors will practically cover most of the foods bass eat or attack. A good bass fly should have the following:

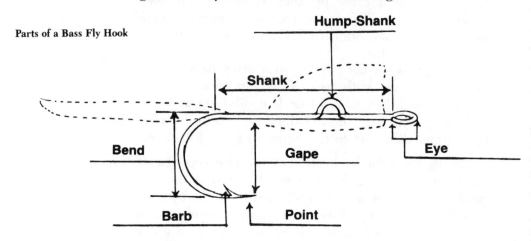

Parts of a Bass Fly Hook

Bass Fly Hook Barb and Point Preparation

1. As manufactured—long, dull, round point and large high barb. Poor hooking at best.
2. Barb bent down and point shortened—sharpened to three cutting edges on the point. Excellent hooking.
3. Optional method. Barb and point filed smaller, with four cutting edges. Excellent hooking and may hold a bit better than 2.

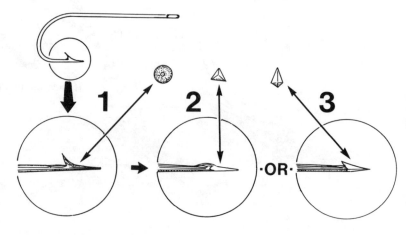

Hook. The hook is the foundation of any good bass fly. Hooks from sizes 12 to 5/0 should be used to assure ultimate hooking performance for each fly size and type. Since the bass's mouth is large and thick, larger and stronger hooks are used than for trout flies. A good bass fly should have a hook that is strong enough not to break or bend under hard use. Its eye should be large and open for easy knot tying of large leaders. Its gape should be large enough to assure a deep bite for good hooking.

Most important is the point sharpness and barb size on the hook. The point must be short and very sharp and the barb very small or nonexistent. Dull points and/or large barbs will seriously prevent hooking most bass, especially on hook sizes 6 to 5/0.

Snag guards. Since bass flies are nearly always used in or near such water structures as tree limbs, cattails, logs, lily pads, moss, tree roots, rocks, and boulders they must be equipped to avoid snagging on these objects. Hangups will cost you flies, fishing time, and fish. So most bass flies should be designed to avoid these hazards yet allow the fly to hook bass well. There are several snag-guard options:

1. *Keel-fly hook*—the fly is tied upside down on the hook shank, which causes it to swim with its point up. In that position it is less likely to hang on objects it passes over.

2. *Bend to hook eye loop*—a loop of heavy nylon monofilament mixed and extended from the hook's bend down below the hook point and back to the fly's head and hook eye. The loop's stiffness supports just the fly's weight but collapses easily when a fish bites down on the fly and exposes the hook point.

3. *Horseshoe loop*—a horseshoe-shaped loop of nylon or wire strands that like the hook-eye loop deflects the fly away or over an object.

The bend-to-hook-eye nylon loop is the most universal design for all six types of bass flies. Here's how to make it:

First choose a strand of *stiff or hard nylon monofilament* about the diameter of the hook's wire or a bit smaller. Tie it onto the hook on top of the shank at the bend, wrapping it down over the upper half of the bend.

Four Types of Snag-Resistant Bass Flies

Bend back or keel hook

Bend to hook eye loop guard

Head horseshoe loop guard

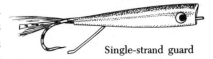

Single-strand guard

90

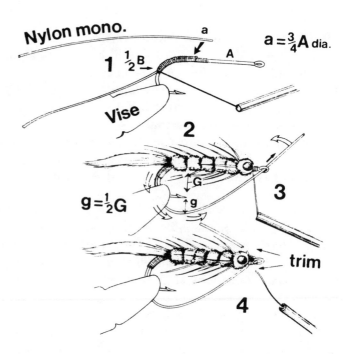

How to make the bend-to-hook-eye loop snag guard.

Next, tie the fly as you normally would but stop and leave a space on the shank immediately behind the hook eye, or where you would normally put the fly's head and whip finish.

Then, pass the nylon strand down around the hook's bend and pass its end up through the hook's eye. Make several thread wraps over the shank and the nylon between fly and hook eye. Adjust loop size so that it extends approximately half the hook's gape distance below or under the hook point.

Finally, bend the nylon strand end back and down over the top of the shank behind the hook's eye and make ten or fifteen thread wraps over the strand and shank. Whip finish the thread and cut excess nylon and thread off. Coat wraps with head cement.

There are always some questions or doubts about this snag guard not allowing the fish to be hooked. But only a small percentage of fish strikes are missed because of it. Usually just the smaller bass and panfish are missed because they cannot get the whole hook into their mouths. This device allows the fly to be fished nearly any place without snagging. Thus you catch many times more fish than you would with a fly without a guard.

Please note that these snag-guard options work best if the fly is pulled *slowly* over objects. Jerking them hard can cause them to fail and the fly hook to snag.

IMITATION AND CHALLENGE

Bass flies roughly fall into two groups—those that imitate or suggest normal live foods and those that suggest live creatures that attract, anger, or challenge a bass. Both groups catch bass better if the following properties are built in.

Action. Made with such materials as soft feathers, hair, rubber strands that breathe or move even when the fly is almost motionless in the water and when animated.

Noise. The fly should have the ability to produce both high and low-frequency water sounds.

Texture. The fly should as nearly as possible duplicate the texture or softness of the live creature it imitates.

Color. Natural imitative colors may be important if the water is very clear but for the most part bass-fly colors should be highly visible or in strong contrasts. Bass respond best to dark colors and bright colors on and below the surface (especially black, white, yellow, and chartreuse). Purple, blue, red, orange, and olive green are rated third; grey, brown, tan, and green seem to be the least effective. Dark colors like black and purple with accents of yellow, red, or white are excellent combinations. Bright white, yellow or chartreuse with accent colors of red, pearl, silver, or gold flash work beautifully.

Flash and sparkle properties of metallic tinsel, mylar tinsel and stripes, tubing, silver, copper or gold-plated hooks and spinner blades provide dramatic eye appeal to any fly. They add lifelike qualities of light reflection and movement that many natural bass foods, especially minnows, possess.

Bass flies that capture air bubbles or cause air-bubble chains to be emitted as they dive or swim under the surface are often more effective than those that do not. Viewed from under water these bubbles have strong light-reflecting properties and contribute to the fly's action or movement as well. These escaping bubbles also emit tantalizing high-frequency sounds.

Bass will sometimes over a period of hours, days, or even months turn on to some unusually hot color or

Five Classic Hard-bodied Surface Popping Bugs

Lefty Kreh's
Potomac River Popper

Loving's
Gerbubble Bug

Peck's Popper

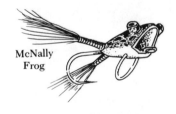

McNally
Frog

Miller Moth Bug

color combinations. Later these will be ineffective. This is best explained because bass will respond to something new or due to an unusual water condition or color situation that make the "hot" color pattern.

Optic effect. Bass and all other sight-feeding predator fish often are excited or triggered to attack a prey if they make strong eye contact with the prey. Bass flies that have highly visible large eyes have a greater attraction than the same flies without eyes.

Odor. A bass fly should have either a neutral or positive natural odor and not offensive odors. A newly manufactured, never fished fly should be considered "filthy and reeking" with offensive manmade odors. Wet and rinse the fly in the water, in vegetation, or in mud where you fish, or treat it with a masking agent or fish-attracting scent for best results.

Bass fly size. Bass flies usually range from ½″ hook, size 12, to 6 or 8 inches, size 5/0. You can cast sizes 12 to 6 on fly-line weights of 5, 6, or 7. Use 7, 8, 9, and 10-weight lines as the flies become larger.

Bass generally prefer larger foods than trout so most popular bass flies are larger than trout flies. Bass can be very size selective, especially if they are predominantly insect and small-minnow feeders. In most cases one, two, or at most three fly sizes are sufficient—small, medium, and large.

Larger bass do seem to prefer larger food forms so large bass flies usually produce fewer but larger bass. However, the small and medium fly sizes are easier to cast and will catch a lot of small, medium, and even some larger bass. Smallmouth and spotted bass generally prefer smaller flies than largemouth of the same weight. This is probably because they have smaller mouths.

Most bass flies need not be made in more than three sizes. Use a small, medium, and large concept as shown here with these shad imitations.

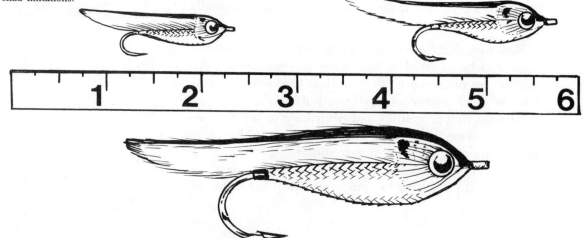

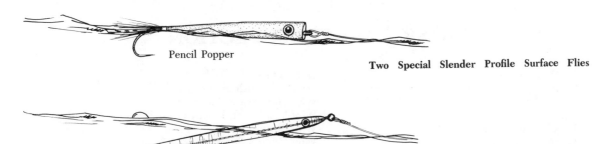

Pencil Popper

Two Special Slender Profile Surface Flies

Quill Minnow

Many of the commercially available Whitlock bass flies are made in these three size ranges to offer the bass fly fisher a practical range of sizes.

One or two dozen assorted bass flies, representing the six fly types, will suffice to start with. At least 50% of them should be floating and floating-diving flies. Well-made bass flies are usually durable and do not wear out quickly. Regularly sharpen the hook points. If the fly has a snag guard and you use a strong leader, you won't lose many flies while fishing. Where pike and pickerel share the water with bass, you must use bite tippets or expect to lose a lot of flies from these aggressive fish, which have sharp teeth.

Be *certain* to allow your flies to dry after you finish fishing them by temporarily storing them on your hat band or vest fly holder.

A BASIC BASS-FLY SELECTION

DRY FLIES
Wulff Series
Dave's Adult Stonefly Series
Humpy Series
Dave's Adult Dragon Fly Series
Hornberg Series
Elk-Hair Caddis Series
Dave's Hopper Series
Dave's Cricket
Bomber Series
Flutter Stone Series

FLOATING FLIES
Peck's Popper Series
Gaines Popper Series
Pencil Popper Series
Hula Popper Series
Whit Hair-Bug Series
McNally Frog Popper
Gerbubble Bug Popper
Whit Mouse Rat
Whit-Hair Gerbubble Bug Series
Sponge Spider Series
Dahlberg Slider Series
Whit Floating Marabou Muddler Series

FLOATING-DIVING FLIES
Whit Diver Frog Series
Whit Diver Snake Series
Whit Diver Minnow Series
Dahlberg Bug Diver
Dahlberg Minnow Diver Series
Dahlberg Hairstrip Diver Series

SWIMMING FLIES
Match the Minnow Series
   (shad, perch, chub, smelt,
   gold shiner, and goldfish)
Lefty's Deceiver
Chico's Seaducer Series
Muddler Minnow
Marabou Muddler Minnow Series
Whit Chamois Leech Series
Woolybugger Series
Grey Ghost
Woolyworm Series
Zonker Series
Lectric Leech Series
Chico's Bend Back Bucktail Series

BOTTOM FLIES
Dave's Crayfish Series
Whit-Hare Water Pup Series
Whit Wooly Leech Series
Whit Shrimp Series
Whit Sculpin Series
Whit Chamois Leech Series
Murray's Helgramite
Whit Helgramite
Whit Stonefly Nymph Series
Whit Dragonfly Nymph Series
Polly's Casual Dress Nymph
Rubber Legs Nymph Series
Troth Bullhead
Whit Bullhead Catfish

JIGS
Whit Eelworm Series
Whit Hare Worm Jig Series
Whit Wooly Leech Series
Whit Chamois Crayfish Series
Whit Chamois Waterdog Series
Whit Chamois Leech Patterns

These flies are commercially available from L.L. Bean and throughout the United States and Canada from fly-fishing shops, general sporting goods dealers, and mail-order catalogs.

The word "series" designates that these flies are available in several sizes and various effective color patterns.

This is only a partial and practical list of flies that can be used to bass fish effectively. Many others are made for local use by both amateur and professional fly tyers and lure manufacturers.

The Whit or Dave prefix indicates that these flies were originally designed by Dave Whitlock.

6
Fly Fishing Bass Flies

Successful fly fishing for bass and associated species requires special techniques and methods. Basically, a fly fisher must *present, control, animate,* and *retrieve* the fly with a tight line, then *strike, hook,* and *control* the bass with aggressive authority. These steps, taken together, make up a precise system that you must understand, practice, and habitually use to fly fish for bass most effectively.

This method is one of the main results of my study to make bass fly fishing as effective as other popular lure methods.

THE WHITLOCK STRAIGHT-LINE SYSTEM

1. Presentation. This system begins with a direct-to-the-water presentation. The forward and down part of the cast must be in a casting plane that causes the fly to hit the target or water immediately after the fly turns over the leader. This gives you the best opportunity to hit the target perfectly. Study the diagram to get a strong mental picture. The overhead or sidearm straight-to-the-water cast will accomplish this best depending upon obstructions, wind, and the direction you must cast from.

2. Rod-tip angle and two-point control. By the time the fly strikes the target you should have two more steps under way. Establish two-point fly-line control as the fly begins to drop to the water and before it actually

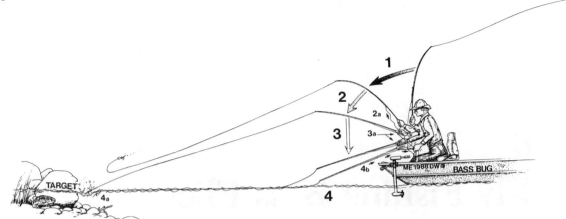

The Straight-Line System

1. Forward-and-down cast stroke in a casting plane so that the fly travels straight to the target.
2. Stop the stroke at a high rod-tip angle and allow the loop to unroll high and directly toward the target.
3. Presentation and rod-tip angle. As the fly strikes the target, begin to lower the rod tip toward the target as the line and leader fall to the water. At the end of this move, the rod tip and line should be next to the water surface.
3A. As the fly falls to the water, begin to establish two-point control with your rod and line hands.
4. Tight, straight line. Pull out any slack leader or line between the fly (4A) and rod (4B) with your line hand. This will create a tight, straight connection between the fly and your rod hand.

hits the water. This is because bass often strike the fly *as* it falls or immediately as it hits the water. *You must be ready.*

3. Rod-tip angle. As the fly hits the water, certainly before all the fly line settles on it, point the fly rod straight at the fly and drop the tip right to the water's surface. This eliminates fly-line slack and premature fly movement that the high rod-tip angle common to trout fly fishing creates.

Because the fly line is heavy, it sags down to a perpendicular angle from the fly-rod tip if the rod tip holds it high; the sag pulls the fly line in, giving you three to five feet of slack line while moving the fly that distance away from the target point. Both results are counterproductive and wrong. So keep the tip low—right at water level.

4. Tight, straight fly line. When the fly, leader, and line come down on the water there will usually be some slack curves in the leader and the line. Keeping the tip low, with your line hand pull in this slack to make as perfect a straight, tight, line connector from your hands to the fly as possible without moving the fly until you

wish it to move. Steps 2, 3, and 4 give you precise control of the fly, to keep it in place, move it, feel a strike, and set the hook most effectively. This straight-line method is the most efficient way to control a bass fly on the water.

5. Retrieving. When the fly lands, you may allow it to rest motionless, let it sink, or begin to animate and retrieve it. To do the latter, maintain the *low rod tip and straight line and use your line hand to make a series of fly-line pulls that will move the fly with whatever animation you wish it to have*. If you have a tight fly line and low rod tip, the fly will move with the exact rhythm and pattern you create by stripping in the fly line with your line hand.

Be sure to maintain your second point of line control by squeezing the line against the rod handle with your rod hand's index finger. When you have retrieved about eighteen to twenty-four inches of fly line, coil it in your palm or drop it and take hold of the flyline at the rod to begin a new retrieve. This is the most efficient way to maintain control of fly-line tension for retrieving and hook-setting with your line hand. Relax your grip slightly as you pull in fly line with your line hand. *Do not use the rod tip to move the fly!* This causes immediate slack line and loss of fly control. Do

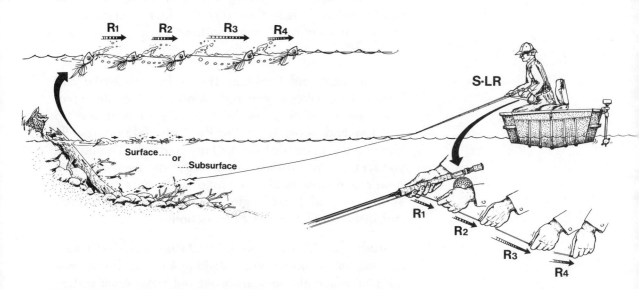

The straight-line system for retrieving surface or subsurface flies. S-LR (Straight-line Retrieve) With your rod low and pointed toward the fly, and the fly line and leader straight, begin line-hand retrieves—R1, R2, R3, R4. The fly will move at the same speed and distance as the retrieve, providing exact control over the animation of the fly.

not use the rod to pull or jerk the fly over or through land or water obstacles; for best results, just continue to use straight line-hand pulls.

6. Strike detection. If your fly remains visible as you retrieve it, you'll see the bass strike it. If the fly is out of sight—under water or at night—you must sense or feel the strike. In most cases, bass will strike hard enough for you to feel this if your fly line is slack-free and your attention is rivetted on it. You may also watch your visible fly line, especially at the point where it is closest to the fly; the line will usually make some movement other than what you are imparting; this can indicate a strike. The fly line may get tight, feel heavy, twitch forward, become slack, or suddenly or slowly move to one side or the other.

Also develop the habit of watching the water when fishing subsurface flies for any abnormal movement or faint flash. Sometimes you will see a bit of water make a swirling eddy near your fly's position. This indicates that the bass is or has rushed the fly, though you do not actually feel it.

In all these cases you must react quickly if you want to hook most bass that take your fly; remember, your fly may look, act, feel, sound, and smell real but most bass quickly become suspicious once they take it into their mouths. Usually they will hold the fly only a second, seldom longer than three or four seconds before they spit it out. It costs nothing to set the hook, a missed fish if you don't.

7. Striking and hooking. Here's how to strike and hook a bass. When you see, sense, or feel the take, *react quickly with a line-hand pull,* with your rod tip still low and pointing at the fly. This tightens the fly line and leader against the fly hook and fish. The instant you feel the fly's resistance, increase the hand-line pull power and also begin to strike with your rod hand. With your rod hand begin the strike by pulling back and lifting with the rod *butt* section.

Study the diagram carefully. *Do not raise or rotate the rod tip* as you do when striking a trout. The fly-rod tip is an efficient shock absorber but *not* a hook-setter. The butt is the shock transmitter and hook-setter that

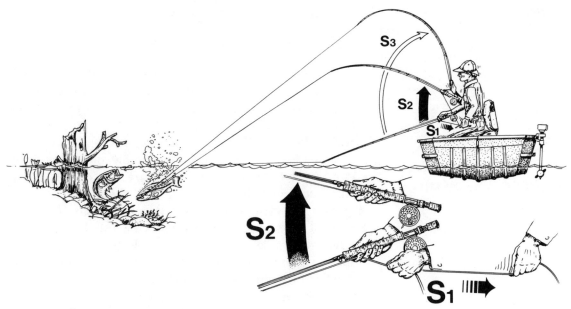

The Straight-Line System for Striking Bass
S1 Begin your strike by tightening the fly line with a line-hand pull.
S2 As you feel resistance, increase line-hand pressure and make a second stroke move. With your rod hand, lift the butt section up and back with considerable force. Note the rod angle in S2.
S3 The most common strike motion for trout and light panfish—but a totally inefficient way of hooking bass on larger flies.

can drive the hook deep into the jaw tissue of a bass. *Don't stop there. Continue a series of short pulling jabs* with your line hand on the line and the rod's butt section. Reason? Bass and other large predator fish use their jaws, teeth, and tongue to hold, bite, and crush any active and sizable creature so it will not be able to escape. Bass, pike, stripers, and snook, even large trout, have tough-skinned bony mouths. For a fly hook to penetrate their mouths you must use a sharp hook with a small barb, or, better, *no* barb. Larger bass fly hooks in sizes 6 to 5/0 with high barbs don't penetrate a bass's mouth deep enough or fast enough because the barb cannot penetrate and hook the bass. Before I realized this problem and discovered a solution, I lost most of the big bass I raised before or during their first jump. This is because they were never really hooked. With barbless and sharp hooks I don't lose a tenth of those big fish now.

Next, these fish are clamping down on what they believe to be a crayfish, minnow, frog, snake, or similar creature so tightly that it is difficult with a fly rod to overcome that bite grip enough to move the fly to hook them.

I have always suspected from observing bass strike flies, then seeing the hooking strike, that actual hooking does not begin until the bass feels the initial strike and decides to spit out the fake. Then, as it *relaxes* its jaw grip, you pull the fly with the line and rod to hook the fish. If this is so, you should line-hand pull the rod strike over a period of several seconds or longer.

Some fish, especially the really big ones that have grabbed a large bulky bass fly, are not easily intimidated and continue to bite and hold the fly for a minute or two before opening up and spitting out the fly— never being hooked. I've often seen this happen with large bass, pike, muskie, pickerel, brown trout, and snook. If your rod tip is not low and if slack line exists, you'll find it difficult to hook a bass.

To test this method, stick the hook of your bass fly into a four or five-pound object—say a cardboard box with sand in it. Place it on a floor, sidewalk, or other smooth surface. Put thirty to forty feet of fly line and leader between the fly rod and the hooked box or object. Tighten the fly line and try to pull and move it to you with the low rod tip, butt, and line-pull strike described in Step 7; *it will move*. Now try to move it with the traditional high-rod trout-fly strike. It's impossible to move it; the rod and fly line absorb most of the strike energy.

8. Fighting the fish. Once the bass is hooked, you must exert enough rod and line pressure to get the initial upper hand. Force the fish to come toward you with fly-line pulls and your fly rod's leverage. When you're sure you have the fish hooked and under some control, begin *with your line hand* to take up any slack fly line between your rod finger's grip and the fly reel by reeling excess slack onto the spool. If you have several yards of slack, it must be put on the reel evenly, with enough tension to avoid tangling problems. Quickly place the fly line with your line hand under your rod hand's small finger and have that finger keep the fly line under control and tension as you reel up the slack. If you have a multiplier fly reel, this can be done two or three times faster.

The sooner you reel up slack, the fewer problems you'll have with line tangles. This is called "getting the fish on the reel." If you cast from a float tube or boat to the shoreline, bass will often come straight at you when

The correct method of holding a fly rod for maximum leverage while fighting a large bass. Note how the extension butt is levered against the waist. The fly reel is being "palmed" for maximum drag control on large, fast fish.

hooked, seeking the safety of deeper water, and you will have lots of slack to recover. Sometimes, however, they will run in the opposite direction and pull out all the slack line. In this case, with slack gone switch immediately to control with the reel. Then fight the fish by taking or giving line from the reel.

Keep these fish away from the various water structures they like so much. The strength of your leader and the stiffness of your fly rod, especially in the butt section, is important in handling this common situation. Keep your rod angled up no farther than ten or eleven o'clock for optimum leverage and shock-absorbing control on the fish. Control of slack is the key to maintaining this optimum angle. If it gets to twelve or one o'clock or farther, you'll lose leverage and line control, and usually the fish.

9. Landing the fish. Because bass have a large, tough mouth and the flies and leaders are usually strong, you can fight them hard with the fly rod. As soon as the bass begins to surface and gasp near you, it's probably ready to land. Now reel the fly-line-leader junction to a point just outside the tip top guide and, using the rod's leverage, slide the bass toward you.

You can now seize the fish in several ways. A dip net is the safest and surest if you use it properly. Place it under the water a few inches, pull the bass over it, then slacken the rod's pull and the bass's head will drop into the net; as it does so, lift the net up. *Never* try to capture or scoop up a bass, as you would an insect in a butterfly net, or you'll lose it.

You can also hand-lip the bass. Most fly fishers prefer this way. Simply grasp the bass by its lower lip and jaw with your line hand's thumb and index finger. This method paralyzes the bass, allowing you to unhook it.

Never hand-lip such species as pike, pickerel, gar, muskie, walleye, bowfin, or large trout because these have long sharp teeth. To hand-land a small muskie, pike, pickerel, or walleye, grip and squeeze it by its cheeks or gill plates. Never poke your fingers into their eyes as this usually blinds them.

Bass, sunfish, walleye, perch, catfish, and stripers have sharp stiff-rayed spines on their backs, sides, or stomachs. Avoid these as you handle them.

ANIMATION AND RETRIEVING

Animating and retrieving a bass fly provides the bass fly fisher pleasure on every cast. No matter how cleverly, cunningly these flies are tied, they're only as effective as how well you place and animate them. *You* are the key to their ultimate effectiveness. The fly-fishing tackle-control system will provide you with the best method to make these flies do exactly what the real creatures do—attract and entice a bass to seize them.

To animate and retrieve bass flies most successfully, follow the straight-line method. *Don't twitch your rod;* this method will cause many feet of slack line to form; you will not feel a strike; and you will lose strikes, particularly from larger fish.

Before you fish any bass fly, observe its water action, floating or sinking or sitting still and under various moves. A well-designed bass fly will look good both dormant and in action. Most bass, especially large ones, are efficient and crafty; they prefer to ambush a helpless or careless creature rather than engage in a tiring high-speed chase of a terrified creature. Most fishermen, on the contrary, like to move lures a lot and fast; that's more entertaining to us I suppose. Practically every big bass I've caught on flies has been when I accidentally (or sometimes on purpose) let the fly sit a long period (ten seconds or more) or moved it *very little* after it hit the water. Other of my better catches were when I was precisely inching the fly in, over, or around structure almost as if I were trying to sneak the fly out of danger. There *are* times when bass will chase and strike rapidly moving flies. Some bass fly-fishing experts even feel fast-moving flies fool larger fish better because such fish don't get a chance to scrutinize the fly, or because the fisherman can cover more water with fast retrieves. If a big bass is in a rare aggressive mood, this will work better; but if this reckless attitude was common to most big bass, there would be few swimming around, since most artificial lure fishermen fish their lures with rapid retrieves.

No one retrieve is always the best. Foods, temperature, water conditions, and individual fish vary. That's why fishing flies and catching bass never gets boring. Don't hesitate to experiment with all types of actions and action speeds.

CONTROL AND RETRIEVE SPEEDS AND OBSTACLES

Before I discuss action/retrieve routines, let me emphasize that to have true control of the fly's movement in still, windy, or flowing water you must: use the low-rod-tip straight-line two-point control system; understand how to *mend* your fly line to keep it and the fly from developing excessive drag movement caused by wind or current; and fish from a stable stationary posi-

Mending a Fly Line to Avoid Wind or Drag

1. The moving water surface pulls a bow into the straight fly line and causes the fly to swim out of direct straight-line control.
2. To correct this, lift the fly rod up until the line is suspended in air; then, without pause, place the line straight and . . .
3. Lower the rod to regain ideal straight-line control again. *Note:* You may have to repeat this mending process if your retrieve is slow or long.

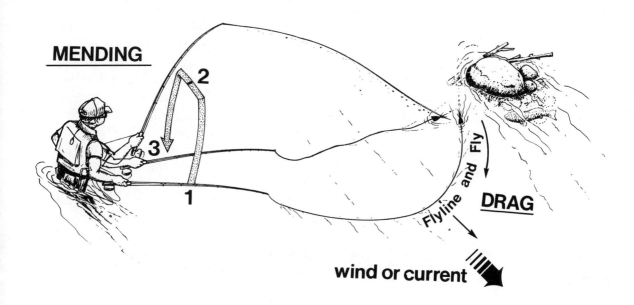

MENDING

Flyline and Fly

DRAG

wind or current

tion. Any time you cast across water currents or a windy surface, that water movement causes drag, which affects your control of the fly. Study this illustration of how to control drag by mending fly line with your fly rod.

Some of the basic bass-fly actions are:

No retrieve. The fly is cast to an exact spot you feel the fish is near. Establish your straight-line control and let the fly float or sink and remain there a good while. This is a particularly good method where the water is clear or fish are pressured or very selective.

Use this method when you suspect a bass is under a structure and put the fly as close to the log, stump, or boulder as you can, and keep it there. It's also ideal if there is just a small open space of water in lily pads, milfoil, cypress stumps, or the like. In these areas the bass will not or cannot move far away for a prey but will respond well to the sitting fly.

My experience with this method has been that the longer you keep the fly sitting the bigger the bass you can expect to catch.

Twitch and pause. Cast the fly to a spot you feel will have a bass near. Let the fly sit in place about three to five seconds, then twitch it an inch or so. Pause and repeat the twitch several times, then make another cast. You want the action of a more-or-less helpless creature or one that's relaxed and moving slightly. If you're using a surface or diving fly, vary the twitch from a silent move to an audible pop or bubble. More noise works best on rough surfaces, and in dark, murky, or densely structured water. This effective method can be used in combination with the no-retrieve method by twitching and pausing *after* you let the fly sit a period of time in the same restricted structure or pocket areas. It's also excellent for moving the fly off and up to and just past an ambush point, such as brush, boat docks, log ends, or a drop-off.

With both methods, watch the water around the fly carefully for any telltale sign of fish movement. These might be a small wake, bubbles, a nervous minnow, a blade of grass or lily moving. Often as you lift the fly for another cast the strike will come to the spot the fly just departed if you fail to see these telltale movements. If this happens, immediately cast back or wait five to ten minutes, then cast. Many times when a bass misses its prey it will become nervous and hide, eventually relaxing and returning to its old ambush position.

Strip and pause. Cast the fly well past where you suspect the bass will be waiting. Let the fly settle a second or two or until it sinks to the level at which you wish to fish it. Now begin a series of fly-line strips, from an inch to a foot long, pausing between them. Vary the strips and pauses—that is, one strip, pause; three strips, pause; one long strip, and so forth. Retrieve the fly up to and past the area you feel holds the bass. The more irregularly cadenced, the more effective this method is. Such a method may indicate natural movements or a handicapped creature. Use this method to fish over and past more extensive structures, such as a series of logs, rocks, stream pockets, moss beds, across points, along creek channels, and so forth.

Panic strip. Cast the fly hard against or past or over the area or structure you feel a bass is near. When the fly lands, begin an immediate series of rapid fly-line strips from inches long to a couple of feet. This fast retrieve usually imitates some food creature in panic. Repeating this retrieve often excites single or groups of fish into a frenzy. This method is excellent for covering lots of open, still, and flowing water where bass are apt to be intercepting and chasing schools of fast-moving minnows. It is also good to "pound" a spot like a reef or flooded timber area with lots of casts to bring deep-water fish to the surface.

These are four basic methods. Obviously, they are only guidelines to animating bass flies but if you practice them and incorporate your knowledge of what the natural food does, where the fish are, and how conditions affect the fish's behavior, you'll have good results.

Be satisfied that you have covered each area you fish correctly and thoroughly. Don't hesitate to change flies or action if you know fish are there. Bass can be psyched into striking if you are clever about retrieving. They'll often respond to repeated casts to the same areas.

Fly fishing uniquely allows the bass fisherman to fish the fly just in the water area where he thinks the bass are, wasting no time reeling in over unproductive water. In other words, you can fish your fly over productive spots two or three times for every one a lure caster can do.

Some days bass will hit *any* fly retrieved *any* way; other days they'll be terribly selective. You must *never become rigid in your thinking* about what flies to fish and how to fish them. Always look for a pattern of behavior on a particular day.

HINTS ON FISHING BASS FLIES

Probably the greatest problem bass fly fishers face is not getting a fly constantly hooked on trees, logs, lilys, cattails, moss, stumps, and rocks. The snag-guard fly is a *must*. Also, always pull the fly over, around, and through these obstructions *slowly*. Pulled slowly, nine out of ten times a fly will escape the snag, because the fly can avoid or crawl over the object without its snag guard bending down. The fly's head, not the hook, will usually engage the obstacle first, stopping it; then if you

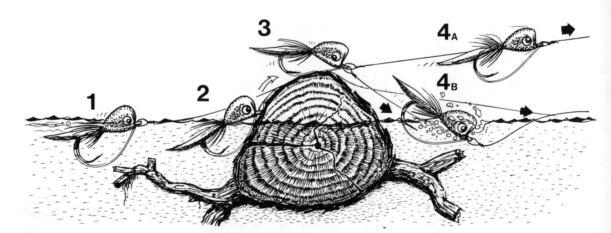

Retrieving a Fly Over Obstacles

1. When the fly is over an obstacle, continue the straight-line retrieve until it contacts the object.
2. On contact, the fly may hang or butt against the obstacle but not actually hook it. *Do not jerk on it with the fly rod*.
3. With your rod held low, calmly resume a steady line-hand pull; the fly will usually slip free and slide over the obstacle without bending the snag guard or hooking the obstacle.
4A. If Step 3 is managed correctly, the fly will come free and drop into the open water next to the obstacle.
4B. If the rod tip is *not* held low, the fly will leap away from the area in which you want it to be.

pull hard, the head will come free but the snag guard
will give and the hook will slam into the object. If you
jerk or move them quickly *with your fly rod,* the fly
will almost always snag the object.

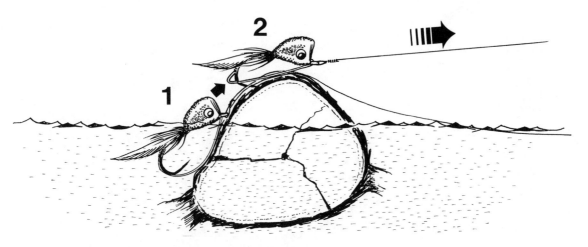

Why Not to Jerk a Fly with a Snag Guard off an Obstacle

1. When the fly touches the obstacle, you'll feel resistance.
2. If you jerk the rod or line with any force, the snag guard will collapse and
   the hook will be driven into the obstacle. If this happens, jerking more
   will only drive the hook deeper or break off the fly.

If you do snag an object, *do not pull hard on it;* in
most cases that simply snags it more. Either wiggle the
rod and fly line to shake the hook loose or make a roll
cast so that the fly-line loop rolls *behind* the snagged
fly, then pull sharply on the line and it will probably
pull the fly off the snag.

If that doesn't work and you cannot reach the fly by
foot or boat, point the fly rod at the snagged fly, tighten
the line, then quickly release it. This sometimes causes
a reverse spring action that will free the fly. If that fails,
again pull the fly line taut with the rod pointed straight
at the snagged fly and continue to increase pressure until the fly tears out or the leader breaks. A lot of fly
fishers use their fly rods to derrick and yank the fly,
hoping it will come free. This violent jerking is seldom
successful and may well damage your rod or line. If
yanking on it does make the fly come free, the recoil
may send the fly rocketing at you or a companion.

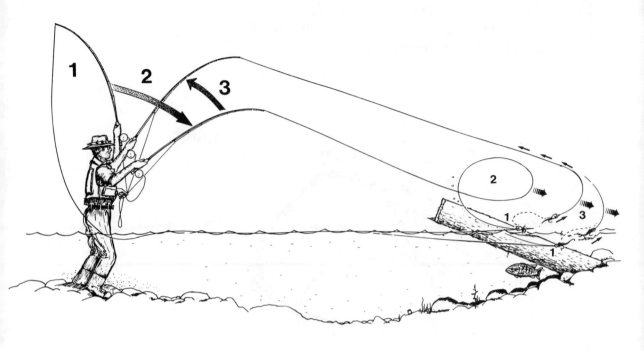

Roll Casting to Release a Snagged Fly

1. Begin the basic roll-cast procedure by adding enough slack line to create a bow of line behind you.
2. Make a forward-and-down over-shoulder casting stroke well above the snagged fly.
3. As the line loop moves over and past the snagged fly, abruptly lift up and back with your rod. This will increase the loop's velocity and pull the fly away from the snag, then back to you.

Note: If the fly is hooked deeply, allow the loop to hit and rest on the water behind the fly. Now jerk the rod up. The added friction of the water will create a long reverse pull, and this will often free a hooked fly.

This modified roll cast can also be used to make a free-swimming fly reverse its direction quickly—which can be a highly effective fishing technique.

SPECIAL METHODS OF FISHING BASS FLIES

Floating fly line—jigging fly. To jig a fly, use a floating fly line and a long leader (eight to ten feet). Allow the jig fly to sink to the bottom or as deep as you wish to fish it. Make a fly line strip, then pause. This causes the fly to hop up and drop down abruptly, or "jig." Bass go crazy over a jig fly that sits on the bottom for two or three seconds then suddenly jigs once or twice.

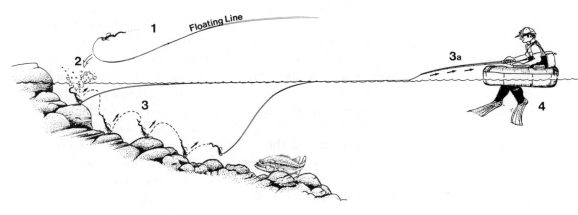

Floating Line and Jigging Fly

1. Cast the jig fly to the target areas.
2. Allow the fly to sink to the bottom. When the leader or line tip stops moving, you'll know it's there. Prepare yourself for a straight-line retrieve.
3. Begin a jigging retrieve with a quick pull-and-pause pattern, to make the fly jig or hop off the bottom.
4. Maintain a stable position with your legs and swim fins as each presentation is jigged over a desired structure.

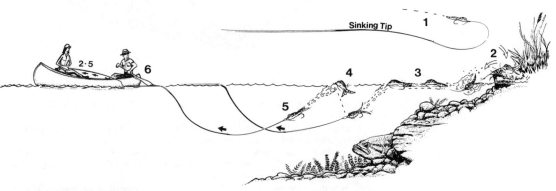

Sinking Tip/Floating Fly

1. Present the fly to a target area on or near the shore.
2. Use a straight-line retrieve and pull the fly into the fishing area . . . as the sink-tip begins to sink.
3. While in shallow water, the fly will be animated at the surface.
4. As the fly moves over deeper water, an abrupt, longer pull on the line will make the fly dive and swim. When you stop pulling, the fly will float to the surface.
5. For a dive and deep-swim action, don't pause but continue to pull the line. Very short swimming pauses will make the fly look like it is wiggling or kicking.
6. The caster's position should be kept stable by the canoe paddler until a cast is fished out.

Sink-tip fly line—floating fly. To obtain a unique floating/diving/subsurface swim-float retrieve, use a sink-tip line and a six-foot leader with any surface or surface-diving fly. Cast and allow time for the sink-tip to sink. When you make short strips on the line, the fly will work on the surface. An abrupt or longer pull causes it to splash or pop and dive following the line tip. Keep pulling and the fly will swim to the depth of the fly-line tip. Stop pulling and the fly will turn head up and return to the surface as long as the line tip does not sink deeper than the leader is long. Such bass foods as frogs, salamanders, turtles, snakes, and minnows have this type of surface-to-surface action.

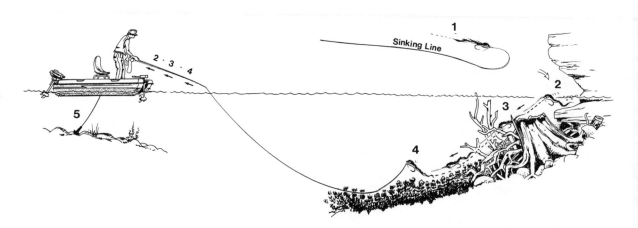

Sinking Line/Floating Fly

1. Present the floating fly on a short leader and full-sinking line to the target area.
2. Pause when the fly lands, to allow the line to sink. In shallow water, the fly may be animated on the surface.
3. As the fly moves over deeper water, retrieving with the sinking line will pull the light fly down; since the fly is so buoyant, it will pass easily through and over most obstacles.
4. When you pause, the fly will float upward the length of the leader. This is a unique and deadly reverse-jigging action.
5. The boat should be anchored—to hold the position while making this special retrieve.

Full-sinking fly line—floating fly. To swim a fly deep over the bottom structure, use two to four feet of leader on a fast full-sinking fly line and a surface fly. The heavy fly line will sink to the bottom, pulling the buoyant fly with it. But the floating fly will suspend off the bottom in relationship to the leader's length and its buoyancy. Each time you pull or strip fly line quickly the fly dives toward the bottom, rising when you stop pulling. If you pull the suspended fly slowly along, it will swim without encountering or hanging over such structure obstacles as moss beds, sunken logs, brush, and rocks. This deadly method is excellent for fishing deep for big bass in heavy brush or weed cover.

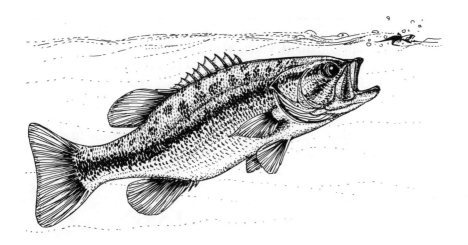

7
Where to Fly Fish for Bass

Smallmouth and largemouth bass are usually eager to accommodate if you offer them the chance to strike your fly. But to have this success, you must be able to pick and approach the areas of lakes and streams where they will most likely be at a particular season, day, and time of day.

Both smallmouth and largemouth do well in lakes and streams. Yet each prefers different areas of these waters.

LOCATING BASS IN LAKES

Smallmouth prefer lake water about 5° to 10°F colder and less silty than largemouth. Smallmouth prefer to live and feed around such structures as rocks, ledges, large boulders, reefs, old submerged stumps, logs, reeds, and open-water leafy plants. They like to spawn over fine gravel or coarse sand bottoms in two to six feet of water near or under an object like a large rock, boulder, clean stump, or log.

Largemouth seek areas almost exactly opposite. They love aquatic and terrestrial vegetation such as flooded shorelines, fallen trees, standing flooded trees, logs, stumps, water lilies, water hyacinth, beaver lodges, cattails, saw grass, pickerel weed, duckweed, floating algae masses, milfoil, coontail moss, and similar features. Any area that looks like a water jungle will attract largemouth bass.

Largemouth prefer to spawn in one to three feet of water over silt, sand, or fine gravel bottoms especially beside or under such structures as fallen trees, logs, stumps, lilies, or manmade objects like duck blinds, boat docks, and fence posts.

Ideal Lake Habitat for Smallmouth Bass

Ideal Lake Habitat for Largemouth Bass

LOCATING BASS IN STREAMS

Both bass seek the same structures and bottom in streams as they do in lakes. The smallmouth, however, prefers to live in fairly fast waters while the largemouth will seek the slowest or deadwater areas.

Look for stream smallmouth in the run area just below riffles, especially if there are lots of large rocks, boulders, and ledges. Ledges along the side of the run and pool will have smallmouth under them. Small islands with good water flow around one or both sides, made up mostly of coarse rock and ledges, are excellent. Log jams at the head of a pool are good spots, especially if the current moves into and beside them. The flat or tail at the end of a pool, where the water speed begins to increase, is an excellent smallmouth feeding area at night and during twilight hours.

Largemouth will live along the shoreline or edge of a run if there are plenty of logs, roots, vines, and overhanging tree limbs to give them relief from the moving water, and places to hide or cover for ambush. Largemouth prefer the wider, deeper, slower areas of pools, especially their shorelines when choked with roots, logs, aquatic vegetation; nice shade lines are a plus.

If the stream has old dead-end channels or sloughs, largemouth will be there, especially around fallen trees, beaver lodges, stumps, lilies, or moss beds, and always under the shady area.

FINDING BASS

Small lakes and streams are usually miniatures of larger lakes and streams. You can locate fish more easily in such miniatures, and approach and fly fish for them better, especially if you're just starting to fly fish for bass.

Try to pick areas that are sheltered from the wind, and those with a shallow average depth and a stable water level. Waters with a high ratio of shoreline to open water are best to fly fish. Deep open water is difficult to fly fish. Natural lakes and streams and/or those that are not constantly manipulated by dams, irrigation demands, metropolitan water use, are more predictable. Fluctuations can affect fish and food behavior and their locations drastically.

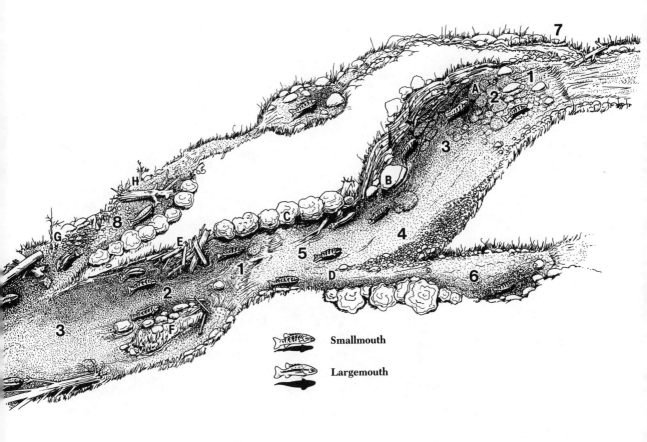

The Most Productive Areas and Structures in a Stream

Areas:

1. Riffle
2. Run
3. Pool
4. Flat
5. Tail of pool
6. Feeder spring or creek
7. Cutoff
8. Slough

Structures:

A. Ledge rock
B. Large boulders
C. Bank shadeline
D. Feeder outlet channel
E. Drift-wood pile
F. Islands
G. Lillies and pickerelweed
H. Old fallen trees

When you first begin to fly fish for bass, especially in new and large waters, it's best to go with someone knowledgeable about the area. Hiring a good bass guide, especially if he fly fishes, is usually time and money well spent. Check with the person and make sure he understands how and what you want to fly fish for; a fly fisher's needs can vary greatly from those of a lure fisherman.

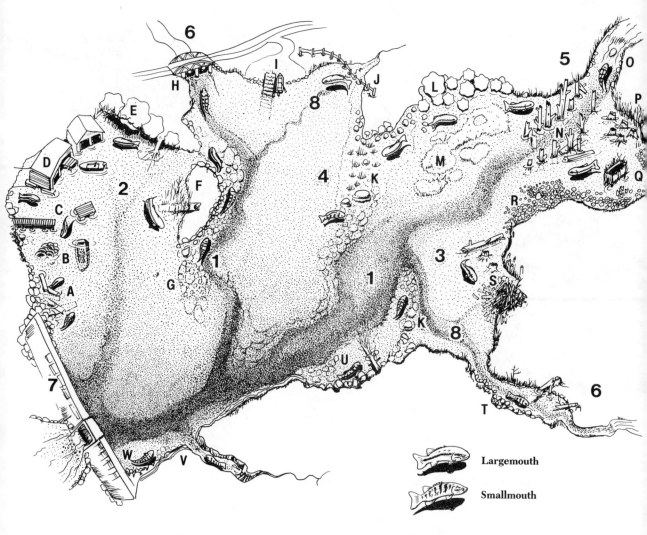

Lake areas and specific structures one to ten feet deep, which large and smallmouth bass prefer and which are excellent for fly fishing.

Areas:

1. River channel
2. Sheltered shallow bay
3. Shallow sheltered cove
4. Long shallow points
5. River and creek inlets
6. First creek pool just above lake
7. Dam rip rap
8. Creek channel

Structures:

A. Log and driftwood piles
B. Old sunken boats, auto-tire fish cover
C. Docks
D. Boat-house docks
E. Tree shadelines

F. Islands
G. Shallow rocky reefs or humps
H. Bridges
I. Boat launch areas and ramps
J. Flooded fences
K. Shallow points with reeds and rocks
L. Water trees and bushes
M. Moss beds
N. Standing and fallen trees
O. Shorelines of inlet area
P. Cattails and tree stumps
Q. Duck blinds
R. Lillies and pickerelweed
S. Beaver and muskrat dens
T. Chunk rock shoreline
U. Steep rocky bluffs and large boulders
V. Deep, narrow cove shoreline
W. Shallow area close to the outflow at a dam

Bass and associated species are also quick to adapt to manmade alterations and structures. Do not be put off by a boat dock sitting in the back of a lake cove, or a wire and post fence staked across a farm pond or a bridge abutment over a smallmouth river pool. These are magnets to bass, each providing cover, a spawning area, or features that attract food.

I watch constantly for man-made bass-attracting structures such as duck blinds, boat docks, jetties, riprap, bridge abutments, sunken boats, old fences, flooded roads, old cars, retaining walls, boat-launching ramps, swimming rafts, culverts, water-supply intakes, and steam-generator plant outlets. Though not necessarily beautiful, these will often be magical hot spots for the most or biggest bass.

You can also improve a local watershed by placing various structures on or near the shoreline in one to ten feet of water. Christmas trees, auto tires, tree trimmings, railroad ties, cinder blocks, barrels, old stumps, and similar objects will improve the shoreline or streamside of waters lacking in good natural bass structure. Probably the best all-around shoreline structure is a fallen, windblown, sawed, or beaver-cut tree.

Always be alert, listening and watching for bass foods and feeding activity.

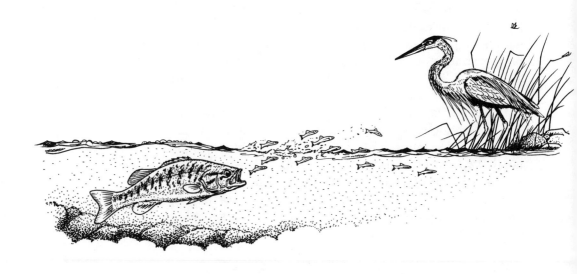

Watch for such clues to feeding bass as excited birds on the shoreline and panicking baitfish.

Very clear water, unless filled with structure, is more difficult to fly fish than water with more color. Colored water and shallow water warms faster in the spring to ideal feeding and spawning temperatures. Twilight and night time are the best fly-fishing times when the water is a bit too warm and when the bass are fished for or disturbed a lot. In waters where there is little shoreline structure cover, such as manmade reservoirs, bass use water depth as a structure substitute for comfort, food, and protection.

When the water level of a lake or stream is abnormally falling, bass become reluctant to stay in shallow shoreline structure areas so look for them in deep water where such structures as ledges, dropoffs, and standing or downed trees are abundant. When water levels are increasing, bass will move into new flooding structures along the shoreline and aggressively feed on almost anything that moves.

For bass to be successful predators, they must consistently tune their instincts to their environment. And to be a successful predator of bass, *you* must be in tune with a bass's predatory lifestyle. As you search for bass, watch and listen for any signs or clues of their presence and activity. Just as important, study the activity of their foods—not just those within casting range but distant sounds and sights as well. A splash, nervous minnows, moving aquatic plants, old bubbles on the water, fishing shoreline birds, a wake or swirl, a faint flash—these and other signs should all be noted. Each day or night on bass water has its particular character; so you must study the water each time you're out, and as soon as possible. Stay alert, open-minded, and flexible—and use your good common sense.

WEATHER AND WATER CONDITIONS

Bass, like most predator fish, are stimulated by changing weather conditions. Approaching fronts, wind, rain, low light conditions such as fog, clouds, and shoreline shade usually make them most active. Long, stable high pressure, bright calm sunny days, and temperatures rising above 80°F or falling below 60°F can make fishing slow. If the water temperature is low, the warmest period of the day will usually provide the best feeding activity; if it's warm, the coolest time of day will be the best time to fly fish.

METHODS OF APPROACH

You can approach bass by walking, wading, float tubing, or boating. Fly fishing requires more unrestricted space than other fishing methods so most fly fishers wade or boat to reach the fish; in most bass waters, the boat is more effective than wading.

Bass fly fishing is best accomplished if the fly fisher can cast and fish from a stationary position. Walking or wading is the simplest answer, and where these are practical, use either. But when it's neither practical nor safe to walk or wade to reach the areas you wish to fish, then float tubes, canoes, rafts, and boats must be used. There is a real revolution in wading and boating equipment designed for bass fly fishers.

Float tubes. The float tube is a truck tire inner tube with a nylon or canvas cover that provides a seat or saddle arrangement plus back rest and storage pockets.

The fisherman sits in the saddle using his feet and legs to move and position himself in the water. Float tubes are practical for reaching areas you cannot wade; because of their low profile and quiet operation, float tubes are extremely good for getting close to bass and having precise fly control.

Most fly fishers prefer to use stocking-foot waders and swimfins to move about. Be sure the fins float or secure them to your waders so you don't lose one. The alternative is foot paddles; though slower and more troublesome, these are more practical if you must frequently stand and walk over shallow areas.

Float tubes are stable and safe to use in sheltered ponds, sloughs, lakes, and *slow-moving* creeks and rivers. *Never use a float tube in fast-moving water.*

Foot-paddle boats are inflatable or plastic molded, pontoon-like boats for one person. They are the next step up from float tubes. Though larger, like the float tube they are still leg-and-foot paddle-powered by the angler who sits on a low platform seat just above the water, with just his lower legs and feet in the water. The advantage of the foot-paddle boat is that it can be moved faster and into shallower underwater structure or obstructed areas. These boats allow the angler to sit more or less dry above the water and carry more equipment. Like the float tube they allow you to get close to bass. The paddle boat, being more stable and larger, can also be fitted with an electric motor or small gas engine that reduces the paddling work and extends the range and water areas. Paddle boats cope with windy surfaces a bit better than the lower-profiled float tubes.

Canoes. Portable cartop twelve to eighteen-foot double-end and square-stern canoes are outstanding, lovely boats to fly fish most small and medium-sized lakes, marshes, and streams for one or two fly fishers. Especially good are those made of low-maintenance, quiet, flexible, and nonsticking hulls of polypropylene, fiber glass, Kevlar, or ABS plastic. Their narrow, shallow-draft bottoms allow you, quietly and smoothly, to penetrate almost any area of shallow water or heavy aquatic vegetation with one or two people paddling. Their low-water profiles allow you to get close to bass without alarming them.

With a stern motor mount or square-stern model you can use an electric motor or small ½ to 7hp gas engine (depending upon canoe size) if you need to travel far or fast. The wide-beam square-stern Coleman sixteen-foot Scanoe is probably the most versatile and universal craft the one-boat bass fly fisher can own. It can be paddled quietly, rowed, poled, or powered with an electric or gas engine.

Cartop bass boat. Cartop or mini bass boats are short, eight to ten feet long, wide, shallow-draft, extremely stable, molded-plastic boats that accommodate one or perhaps two fly fishers. They have comfortable raised swivel chairs for ultimate back and leg comfort and are stable enough to allow one fly fisher to stand and fish. The mini bass boat, like the float tube and foot-paddle boat, should be considered primarily for ponds, sheltered lakes, and slow rivers. For power they have a bow and stern electric-motor bracket; the stern will accommodate a small gas engine. Because they have a wide, flat bottom, they are stable and can be used in shallow water. But this hull's drag requires the use of a motor for locomotion. Though cartopping is possible, most of these boats are better hauled in pickup beds or larger station wagons, or dock stored when you use them.

John boats. The economical metal or fiberglass square-bow or modified V-bow wide-beam flat-bottom John boats ten to sixteen feet long are superb fly-fishing boats. They are comfortable, stable boats and permit two anglers to sit or stand while fly casting. Their unique hull designs and low profile make them easy to use in the wind; and they can comfortably reach shallow areas of lakes, streams, bays, and flats. They make excellent boats for floating streams. Their keeled flat bottoms allow them to be powered upstream with smooth ride and positive control with outboard motors and over shallow shoals and riffles.

Use oars, pole, or electric motor on them for the best position control. John boats, especially small ones, are *not good for rough windy water*.

Drift boats. The McKenzie-style drift boat is excellent for large stream or river bass fly fishing. They are for two or three persons, one rowing while one or two fishers stand or sit to fly fish from the bow and the stern.

The McKenzie drifter allows precise approach and control while fishing the riffles, runs, and pools of high and low-gradient rivers. They are superior to the John boat in rough turbulent waters, though the John boat is superior if you need to use a gas engine for moving up and down river. These boats require a trailer winch to transport and to load and unload them.

Bass boats. The modern fiberglass or metal bass boat is a roomy, stable, expensive, bass-fly-fishing platform. It is particularly useful for big, open-water lakes and large rivers, tidal bays and flats, and to go long distances fast and comfortably. The metal modified-V John-boat-hull bass boat is considerably lighter and less expensive than similar length fiberglass bass boats. Usually the metal bass boat is a better choice for most bass-fly-fishing requirements, and more economical.

Though bass boats are reasonably shallow draft, their height, size, weight, and power requirements make them less desirable for stalking bass with a fly rod in close and thick structure. The clutter of electrical equipment, fishing chairs, electric motor, large outboard motors, and whatnot, can tangle lines, so their decks must be modified and cleared for the fly fisher.

EQUIPMENT AND ACCESSORIES FOR BOATING

Anchors are important for holding your position, for precise fly control, especially if you are alone with wind or stream currents. Drag and sea anchors will slow down your boat's drift in excess wind. If you use a drag anchor in a stream, be sure to use it only on a boat's bow and have it rigged for quick release should it hang up in a treacherous area.

Paddles allow you to make precise and quiet position moves; and they provide emergency locomotion should your engine fail. No boat you fly fish from should be without one. Though electric motors save us a lot of physical work and are popular with boat fishermen, they have limitations for lake and stream fly fishing. Their noise alerts fish to your presence; in water full of aquatic vegetation, brush, and stumps, they are difficult to operate, and a paddle seldom fails. Electric motors do not properly control or move a boat in swift water. Paddles and oars are irreplaceable for controlling most boats for the best fly-fishing methods in most areas.

They require neither heavy batteries nor gasoline to operate.

Poles are useful accessories for precise anchoring or locomotion in shallow areas of lakes, swamps, bays, flats, and rivers.

Fish locators such as the electronic flasher and graph fish locators are useful tools to the bass fly fisher for locating specific submerged structures bass and associated fish will gather on. They are especially good in large, open-water areas for determining depth, structures, and fish concentrations. Such areas are nearly impossible to read by eye or map without a locator. I find them particularly useful in water I don't know and at night.

NOTES ON BASS-FLY-FISHING BOATS

Set up your boat so that it will be as quiet and efficient as possible. Rubber or vinyl mats or outdoor carpeting on the floors, seats, and decks cut down fish-alarming noises. Keep your boat as uncluttered as possible so excess fly line will not hang or tangle on objects. If you buy an electric motor to fly fish with, the hand-operated models are far superior to those operated by foot, for more reasons than there is space here to discuss.

Approaching an area at a correct boat angle can affect how well you cast and present your fly to a bass. Whenever possible, position the boat so that the bow is at an angle and side that allows you to make both the sidearm and underhand cast as well as the overhand cast. This means that when moving along the shoreline a right-handed caster should have the shoreline on his left-bow side and a left-handed caster the shoreline to his right-bow side.

If the boat has two or more persons in it, keep it moving parallel to the shoreline, not perpendicular; this simple rule keeps hooking accidents to a minimum.

If two fly fishers fish a shoreline on the same boat side at the same time, and one can cast left-handed and the other right-handed, put the right-hander on the right side in the stern and vice versa. Now both can use the sidearm cast and keep their fly lines and flies safely apart from each other.

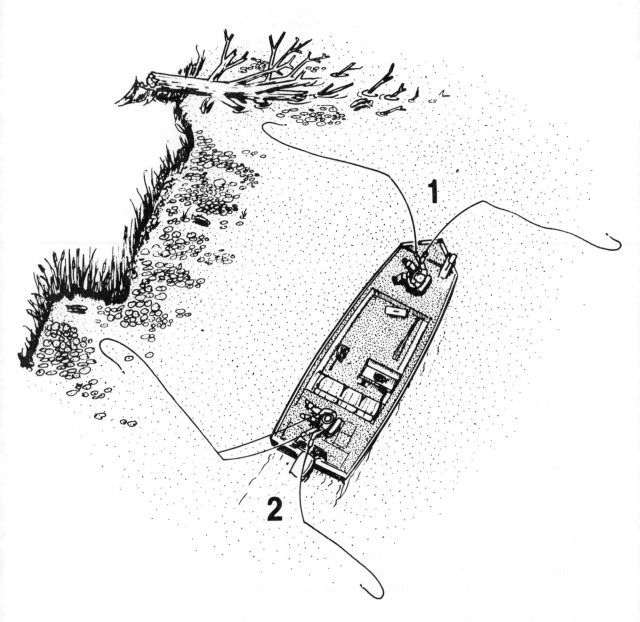

The correct boat angle for best efficiency and safety when fishing to shore-lines and various structures.

1. The right-hand caster in the bow fishes left to the shorelines with over-the-shoulder, side-arm, and underhand casts for safety and efficiency.
2. A left-handed caster fishes from the stern for the same advantages and can use different angles of presentation than the right-handed caster, fishing from the bow. A right-handed caster fishing from the stern can use an over-the-shoulder and back side-arm cast here. The bass boat is con-trolled from the stern with an electric motor.

TEAM WORK AND MORE FISH

When two people share a boat and both are trying to fly fish at the same time, the boat is seldom in good position or control. It's much more efficient to have one fish and the other control the boat. You will be able to make more accurate casts, keep quieter, and hook and land larger fish with this team system. At reasonable intervals, change places. This method of fly fishing for bass is the most efficient. Each fish caught is really caught by the team.

STEALTH

It's more productive to get close to bass than it is to make long accurate casts to them. The closer you get to a bass the more casts you can make, the better your accuracy, the more fly control you'll have, the better you can detect strikes and hook fish, and the more fish you will land. When you walk, wade, float, or boat, keep a low profile and be quiet. Wear clothing that blends with the background and light conditions. Use more sidearm casts. Keep as quiet as possible in the boat as you use the paddle, oars, pole, electric motor— and use them as little as possible.

If bass are not aware of your presence, they are far more apt to strike any fly you offer than they will strike the best fly if they are alerted to or disturbed by your presence. So take your approach to bass water as seriously as you do your tackle balance, casting, and flies. When a bass takes your fly, though, yell and laugh as loud as you want!

8
Fly-Fishing Safety

The most common safety hazards when fly fishing for bass are sunburn, insect bites, stings, accidental falling, being accidentally hooked, fish bites, cuts or punctures, boating accidents, and drinking bad water. Reasonable care and attention will help you avoid these hazards.

Hooking. Whenever you or a companion is fly fishing, wear a wide-brim or long-billed fishing hat, glasses, a long-sleeve shirt, and pants. These will give you almost complete protection from being hooked.

Know where everyone is located and don't cast in each other's path. Always assume the dual responsibility to keep out of the way of another caster and to keep your casts away from others. Always hold your fly in hand; release it only as you begin to cast. This avoids hooking yourself.

Wind is a hooking hazard, especially to oneself. Watch the wind's effect on your fly and line, and position yourself and your casting stroke to keep the fly safely away from yourself and others.

When fly fishing from a boat, keep the boat and your cast in such a position that they will prevent the hooking of your companion or yourself.

Be careful when trying to pull a snagged fly loose from an object above or at water surface level. When it comes free under tension, it may come fast and straight, right at you!

Always use barbless bass flies; the barb serves no practical purpose and barbless hooks are simple, fast, and painless to remove from your clothes, skin, and the mouths of fish. Unfortunately, most bass fly hooks have barbs, but you can easily mash them down with pliers or file them off.

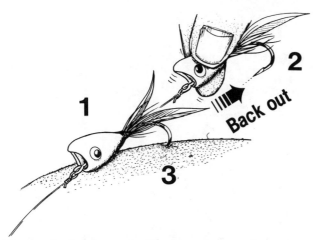

Removal of Barbless Hooks

1. The fly is stuck in clothing or skin.
2. To remove, simply back the hook out the opposite direction it entered.
3. If the wound bleeds, let it do so and then apply an antiseptic ointment and bandaid.

If you do hook yourself or someone else, there are several ways to remove the hook safely. First, if it is a barbless hook, just grasp the fly and remove it by reversing the entry path. If the hook has a barb and this has penetrated the skin, the situation is more serious. First, don't panic. Ninety-nine percent of all hooks can be painlessly and quickly removed. If someone is with you, let him remove it; if you are alone, you can do so if the hook is easily reached by both hands. If not, cut the leader tip off the fly, and seek help elsewhere.

Should the fly be lodged in your eye socket area, or buried in your skull bones or in your throat or neck, go *immediately to the emergency room of the nearest hospital*.

Here are steps to follow when you decide that you or a companion should remove the hook: First, cut off the leader at or near the fly, and put your fly rod aside; second, determine if the hook is buried or has turned and exited your skin. Most hooks will simply be buried. If it is buried past the bend, follow Procedure A. Follow Procedure B if it has exited back out.

Procedure A (for a hook buried past the barb). Take a section of heavy nylon monofilament or other fishing line or fly line, long enough to secure a firm handhold on it when it is doubled. Pass this through the hook bend and back toward the direction opposite where the hook entered. With your other hand, press down the hook eye (fly-head area) with your index finger or thumb against the skin. While pressing down on the hook eye, make a straight, smooth, quick, firm pull on the doubled line away from the direction the hook entered. The fly will pop out without pain or tissue dam-

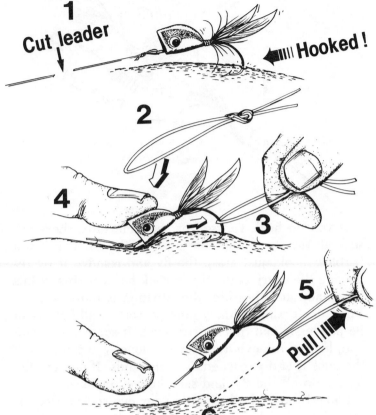

Removal of Barbed Hooks (Procedure A)

1. If the barb has deeply penetrated the skin, start by cutting off the leader close to the fly.
2. Pass a loop of strong nylon monofilament over the head and body of the fly.
3. Position the loop around the bend of the hook and hold it (as shown) with your fingers.
4. With your thumb or index finger, press down on the eye of the hook (near the head of the fly). This assists in aligning the hook with its entry path.
5. While pressing down on the hook eye, make a quick, short pull on the loop in the opposite direction than that in which the hook entered. The hook will pop out, safely and painlessly.
6. Bleed and treat the wound with antiseptic and a bandaid.

age. Some bleeding may occur, but that will help flush the wound. Encourage the bleeding a while, then stop it by applying direct pressure.

Procedure B (for a hook that is turned back out). This removal method can only be attempted if you have a pair of side-cutting diagonals (dikes) or pliers. If you don't, go to the emergency room of a hospital or to a physician for assistance. Check the hook to see that the barb has cleared the skin. If it has not, push it on out. (Most hook pain can be avoided by applying ice to the area until it is numb—and then pushing the hook through the skin.) Cut off the point and barb with side-cutting pliers and remove the debarbed hook by backing it out along the same path by which it entered.

In either case, treat the wound with antiseptic and cover it temporarily with a sterile bandage. As soon as convenient, consult a physician about the need for a tetanus shot.

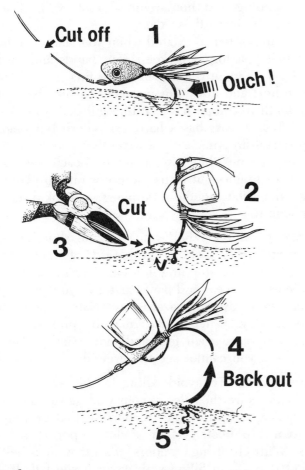

Removal of Barbed Hooks (Procedure B)

1. Here the barbed hook has penetrated the skin and turned. Start, as before, by cutting off the leader near the fly.
2. Now grasp the fly and push the point and barb through the skin until the barb is completely exposed.
3. With wire-cutter pliers, cut the hook just behind the barb.
4. Now back the cut hook out through the skin.
5. Allow the wound to bleed thoroughly, then apply antiseptic and a bandaid.

Sunburn. Wear protective clothing and hat with wide brim or long bill. Use sunblock cream or lotion, especially on your face, nose, ears, and lips.

Insect bites. Most insect bites can be avoided by wearing the same protective clothing you use against the wind, sun, and hooking, and by the frequent use of insect repellant. Wind and smoke discourage a lot of flying biting insects. Burrowing biters such as ticks and chiggers can be avoided by staying out of weedy areas, and by careful body inspection and bathing with lots of soap.

Fish bites. Fish bites, cuts, or punctures are common hand injuries. What causes them are a fish's sharp teeth, sharp gill-plate edges, and spined fins. Some of these wounds are painful, occasionally infectious, and even poisonous. Use precautions when landing and handling any fish. A dip net, a tailer, a gaff, and various mouth-opening and hook-removal tools will, if used properly, eliminate these dangers.

First, do not get so excited when you land or unhook a fish that you forget to keep your hands and fingers away from its mouth, gill plates, and fins. Learn which fish can hurt and how. For instance, all pike have long sharp teeth but none have cutting gill plates or sharp-spined fins. A bass has a harmless mouth but needle-sharp dorsal-fin spines.

Whenever possible, use a net or beach your fish. Keep your fingers out of its mouth or off gill plates by using a hemostat, needle-nose pliers, or hook disgorger to unhook it.

Walking safety. When you walk the shoreline of a lake or stream *be alert* to the hazards of stepping in a hole, tripping, or stepping in a boggy spot. Look, then step. Wear footwear and pants that give you ample protection against existing hazards, especially in poisonous-snake country. When snakes may be present, watch where you place each foot and move slowly. Do *not* step where you cannot see the ground.

Safe wading. To avoid falling in the water as you wade, make sure the soles of your wading shoes, boots, or waders give you ample traction for that bottom. If you wear hip boots, never wade deeper than your knees. With chest-high waders, *always* wear a belt to prevent them from filling with water if you fall. If you are wading in murky water, swift water, or over irregular or slick bottoms, use a wading staff for safety. Polaroid glasses are useful while wading in clear water because they cut glare and allow you to see obstacles on the bottom. Never jump into murky water or wade from a bank dock or boat before checking the depth with your wading staff, paddle, or even fly rod. If you can't swim, or swim poorly, always wear a life vest or flotation vest when you wade. *Do not* wade where there is boat traffic. If you wade below dams, be alert to water speed and height fluctuations.

Safe boating. Most boating accidents associated with fly fishing can be avoided by observing local boating rules. Do not take your float tube or boat into hazardous water or use excessive speed where waves or obstructions may cause you to capsize or sink. Always wear life preservers while moving across water. Keep

Always observe the posted regulations on any lake or stream you fish.

your boat bottom neat, clean, and free of foot hazards. Avoid standing up in small boats, canoes, or V-bottom skiffs. Do not wear your waders while boat fishing. Do not anchor your boat or use drag anchors in turbulent rivers or tidal flows. Always be alert to such special dangers as poisonous snakes and alligators; avoid them and the areas they frequent, especially when wading, float tubing, and in small boats.

USEFUL ACCESSORIES

Polarized sunglasses—reduce glare and allow you to see through the water much better.

Broad brim hat with fleece band—for head protection and bass-fly storage.

Fly-fishing vest—useful method of carrying most flies and accessories when walking, tubing, and wading.

Fly tackle box—when boating, the most convenient way to carry your flies, reels, leaders, tools, and other small gear.

Wading staff

Hemostat

Knot kit

Clipper

Bug and fly flotant

Compass

Pliers

Bite tippet

Waterproof matches and butane lighter

Insect repellant

Water thermometer

Wader patch kit

Sunblock and lotion

Lip balm

Adhesive strips and antibiotic cream

Ziplock bags and paper towels

Scale and tape measure

Dip net

Whistle

Raingear

Loop of line for hook removal

Soap

Snake and insect bite kit

9
Bass and Associated Fish

Here are brief profiles of the various bass and more important species that often share bass waters and are likely to strike bass flies.

Kentucky or spotted bass.

Smallmouth bass.

Largemouth bass.

LARGEMOUTH BASS (Micropterus salmoides), sometimes called green trout, green bass, and lineside bass, prefer to live in lakes and streams in depths of one to twenty feet that are filled with various aquatic and terrestrial vegetation. A largemouth has a very large mouth (bucket mouth); its upper jaw bone extends well past the point of its eye. It has a green to brown back, with a dark, irregular stripe from its eye to its tail; it has a yellow to white stomach.

Largemouth average 1½ to two pounds and often grow to eight to ten pounds in good habitat, especially in their southern range, southern California, and Florida. The Florida subspecies and hybrids of it now also exist in other southern and western waters. They look like the largemouth bass, are long lived, and often exceed sixteen pounds in good habitat.

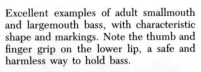

Excellent examples of adult smallmouth and largemouth bass, with characteristic shape and markings. Note the thumb and finger grip on the lower lip, a safe and harmless way to hold bass.

This photo shows the size difference in the mouths and upper jaw bones of a largemouth and smallmouth bass. The largemouth's jaw bone extends past its eye, the smallmouth's just *to* its eye.

Bass have small, harmless, sandpaper-like teeth in their upper and lower lips.

SMALLMOUTH BASS (Micropterus dolomieui) are a close second to the largemouth in popularity and range. Though smallmouth do not average as large (½ to ¾ pound smaller) or reach the maximum size of the largemouth for a given age, smallmouth do fight with more speed, strength, and endurance. Unlike the largemouth, smallmouths fight harder the larger they get. Smallmouths from three to six pounds are considered large; eight to ten-pounders are rare.

Because they prefer food and water similar to trout, especially brown trout, smallmouths are the ideal bass for which a trout fly fisher should start bass fishing. Smallmouth often share the lower and somewhat warmer stretches of cold rivers with brown trout, rainbow trout, and landlocked salmon.

The smallmouth bass is easily distinguished from the largemouth by its smaller mouth; the jawbone only extends even with its eye; and the fish has a series of irregular vertical back and side bands or blotches. Its back is usually dark olive-brown or dark golden-brown, shading to gold or yellow on its sides and with a silvery grey belly. The smallmouth's scales are smaller than those of the largemouth and its tail is a bit larger; it has a more distinct point at the ends.

Smallmouth bass

The northern smallmouth bass (sometimes called black bass or brown bass) is the most widely distributed but if you fish the small and medium-sized spring-fed streams that feed into the Arkansas River in Oklahoma, Arkansas, and the Missouri Ozarks, you may also catch the troutlike Neosho smallmouth bass (*Micropterus Velox*), known locally as brownies. It has a more slender and torpedo-like shape, smaller scales, and is a beautiful golden-olive to yellow-gold, with faint smallmouth body markings.

SPOTTED BASS (Micropterus punctulatus) or Kentucky or spotted Kentucky bass are an often-confused third bass species that resemble a largemouth in body color and smallmouth in head and body shape. It looks like a cross of the two bass but is not.

The spotted bass usually has more distinctive back and side markings and a more vivid horizontal stripe than either the smallmouth or largemouth. Its coloration is cleaner, and it sometimes has a distinctive blue-green cast to its back and sides. It prefers food, water, structure, and temperature types exactly in between those preferred by the largemouth and smallmouth bass.

The spotted bass averages about ten to twelve inches; three to four-pound fish are exceptional; but it has the better strength and fighting characteristics of the smallmouth bass. Its range is limited, occurring naturally in the Ohio Mississippi drainage from about Ohio then south to the Gulf and then west to Texas, Oklahoma, then east to western Florida. It seems to resist manmade environmental problems, such as fishing pressure, better than the smallmouth.

In recent years the spotted bass has been experimentally introduced to some western states with early success.

REDEYE BASS (Micropterus coosae) are similar in color and shape to smallmouth. It prefers small streams and rivers to lakes and it averages a length of eight to ten inches and about ¾ pound. It exists in upper tributaries of the Alabama and Chattahoochie rivers and tributaries in Alabama; the Savannah River in Georgia; the Chipola River in Florida; and the Conasauga River in southern Tennessee.

The shoal and flint river bass are two additional forms of the redeye that occur in streams of Alabama.

Redeye are similar to the smallmouth in their preference for stream habitat and similar foods.

SUWANNEE BASS (Micropterus notius) are a lovely redeyed native of Florida. The Suwanee is a river bass that is shaped, marked, and colored like the spotted and redeye bass except that it has a distinctive blue or blue-green cast to its lower head and belly area. It seldom grows larger than ten to twelve inches but may exceed two pounds. This fine gamefish prefers the stream channel to shoreline cover and its fight is equal to that of the smallmouth. You will most likely catch Suwannee in the Sante Fe River, Suwannee River, and Withlacoochee River in Florida on small subsurface flies that imitate minnows and aquatic insects.

GUADALUPE BASS (Micropterus treculi) are a small species located only in Texas. It is found in the Colorado, San Antonio, and Guadalupe River systems of south central Texas. This little bass, usually less than twelve inches long, is quite handsome; it has vivid vertical and horizontal patterns of dark bands and stripes. It prefers small stream pools and mostly eats insects and minnows. This fine subsurface fly-striker fights and jumps very well. It lives in the same areas with the largemouth bass but is generally easy to distinguish from its larger relative.

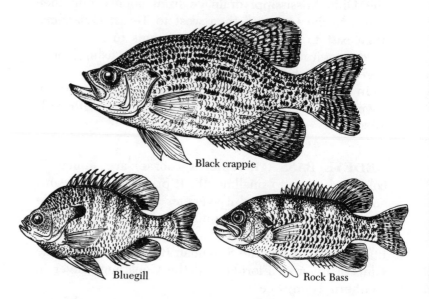

Black crappie

Bluegill

Rock Bass

SUNFISH FAMILY (Centrarchidae) Along with the bass listed, there are at least ten to fifteen species of sunfish that live in the same waters with these bass and will eagerly hit the same flies you use while fly fishing for bass. These sunfish run four to eight inches in length and are part of a group of freshwater gamefish called panfish because of their size, abundance, and excellent food value. Most of these sunfish are hard-striking, hard-fighting gamefish.

Group I. Bluegill, redear, longear, coppernose bream, redbreast sunfish, and *pumpkinseed* are all saucer-shaped, brightly colored, vividly marked, widely distributed sunfish, often called bream or perch in the Midwest and South. They prefer ponds, small lakes, shallow, sheltered areas of large lakes and slow-moving streams. They use the same structures to hide and feed near as bass do. They will be found in shallow water in small scattered groups and in small dense schools in deeper water. Most average about five or six inches, or "hand size," and seldom exceed one or two pounds. Those that do exceed 1½ pounds are fine fly-rod tro-

phies. These sunfish have small mouths and therefore
prefer smaller foods, especially insects, worms, and
minnows. However, they do have plenty of moxie and,
given half a chance, will attack a bass hairbug bigger
than them in size. Use lighter lines, leader, and bass
flies with hook sizes 12 to 6, subsurface and surface, for
most consistent results for these fish. A small dropper
fly tied off a larger bass fly is a deadly way of catching
these sunfish as you fish for larger bass. To avoid them,
use larger bass flies with the nylon-loop snag-guard and
fish over deeper water.

Group II. *Black crappie* and *white crappie*, sometimes called *strawberry bass, specks,* or *calico bass,* are
lovely, excellent eating, larger schooling sunfish than
those in Group I. They prefer the deeper water (four to
fifteen feet) of ponds, lakes, and slow streams, especially where the underwater terrestrial and plant structure is dense. Crappie average about eight inches long
and will often exceed two to three pounds when habitat
and food are right.

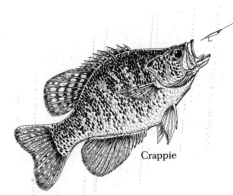

Crappie

**Small Dropper-Fly Rigs for Group 1
Sunfish**

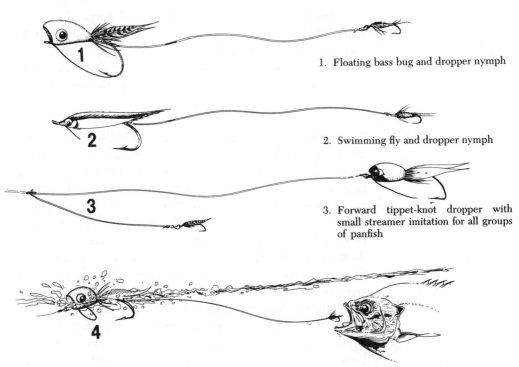

1. Floating bass bug and dropper nymph

2. Swimming fly and dropper nymph

3. Forward tippet-knot dropper with
   small streamer imitation for all groups
   of panfish

4. The action of a larger bass fly often at-
   tracts panfish to the smaller dropper
   fly.

Crappie are primarily minnow and insect feeders; they prefer slow-moving subsurface flies, light colored. They feed at night as well as during the day. Usually crappie will not move far in any direction to chase a fly and normally strike it very gently. However, at spring spawning time they appear to be more aggressive. Crappie have large but tender mouths and must be fought and landed with delicate care or the hook will tear out. Never try to lift a large crappie out of the water by holding just the leader; its weight will usually tear the hook from its mouth.

Both black and white crappie are shaped alike but the black crappie will be darker, with a speckled pattern on its sides, while the white crappie will be lighter and have a vertical speckled pattern on its sides. Though not reputed for their fight, the black crappie fights a little harder than the white and will on occasion tailwalk and jump.

Group III. Green sunfish, rock bass, warmouth bass are aggressive sunfish, shaped like fat bass or groupers; they have very large mouths. They average about six inches and will reach 1½ to 2½ pounds. They are widely distributed in larger ponds, lakes, streams, rivers, and prefer the foods and habitat that resident bass prefer. Like bass, they strike all sorts of surface and subsurface flies without hesitation—often large bass flies, longer than themselves.

Note: All these sunfish, and of course bass, have harmless teeth. Beware of their sharp dorsal-fin rays and handle them all carefully.

PIKE FAMILY (Esocidae) members include the chain pickerel, northern pike, and muskie. They are all exceptional, abundant, aggressive cohabitants in many bass lakes, streams, and swamps. Though all prefer calm waters, all will utilize flowing water if food and water temperatures are suitable. Pike prefer water one to twenty feet in depth and structure types more like those of the largemouth than the smallmouth but they like cooler water temperatures than either bass. They are primarily ambush feeders who live in heavy structure rather than open water. Pike are principally fish eaters but will readily strike almost any surface or subsurface fly that resembles live food. All have numerous long sharp teeth that will easily cut a regular leader so

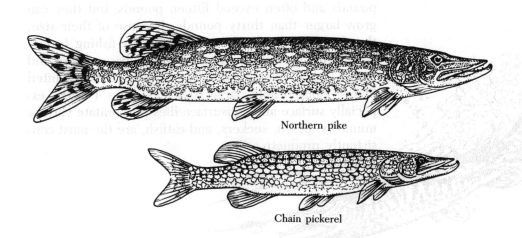

Northern pike

Chain pickerel

you must use bite tippets for them. The pikes are aggressive and fast but because they lack maneuverability in their body design they are best caught on flies that swim in straight lines and regular movement patterns. They normally make exciting, vicious strikes, especially on surface or fast-moving floating-diving flies. Pike prefer to feed in the morning and at midday; they are seldom caught after dark.

CHAIN PICKEREL (Esox niger) are the smallest of the three pikes. They average about a pound; three to four-pound pickerel are exceptional and any over seven pounds are rare. Despite their size they are the most

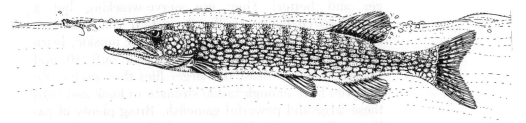

exciting and entertaining of the pikes to catch on a fly rod. No freshwater fish strikes a fly faster and harder. Their range extends from southeastern Canada to Maine to Florida to southeast Texas and north to the Great Lakes. The best large pickerel areas are coastal ponds and brackish creeks. They jump and they fight very well, especially when they reach two pounds or larger.

NORTHERN PIKE (Esox lucius) average five pounds and often exceed fifteen pounds; but they can grow larger than thirty pounds. Because of their size, they are always exciting to hook on fly-fishing tackle. Northern pike live in most northern bass waters and many larger rivers and lakes in the central United States. Long-profile, large bass flies, sizes 4 to 5/0, especially surface and subsurface flies that imitate various minnows, perch, suckers, and catfish, are the most consistently productive flies.

MUSKELLUNGE (Esox masquinogy), especially over fifteen pounds, are probably the most demanding freshwater trophy you can catch on a fly rod. This is because even though they grow to sixty pounds or more, most muskies over fifteen pounds are solitary, rare, intelligent, strong, and demanding predators of larger food forms. Most fly-rod-caught musky are taken accidentally while bass fishing. Deliberately pursuing them is a real task and challenge! Muskies respond best to bass flies that *look big and are actively moved long distances*. This means a lot of long *accurate* casts to precise musky hangouts with lots of challenging fly animation.

Muskies will often follow a fly up to the rod tip without striking it, as if to ask you if you have anything bigger and better! They are nerve-wracking but a marvelous challenge on the fly rod. If you decide to concentrate on fly fishing specifically for muskie, learn their hangouts and use heavier fly tackle of 9, 10, and 11-weight sizes to cast the larger flies they prefer. Be sure you have enough tackle strength to hook and fight these large and powerful gamefish. Bring plenty of patience. You may fly fish a season before you catch your first legal-size muskie (thirty or more inches) but they are worth the pursuit. Their range is similar to that of the northern pike except not as far north into Canada as northern pike range. Muskies usually do not do as well in waters heavily populated with northern pike.

Note: Remember that the pikes have long, sharp, and numerous teeth—so keep your hands away from their mouths and gill filaments.

TEMPERATE BASS FAMILY (Perchichtyidae). This group of open-water lake and large-river school fish are excellent for the fly rod. They strike bass flies, especially those that imitate school minnows, very well. This group of fish are generally robust, strong, and hard-fighting, though they seldom jump. They tolerate cold and warm water well. They all spawn in the spring, preferring the fast waters of rivers or major lake inlets to scatter their eggs. During their spawning runs and when they feed in water two to ten feet deep, they are easily caught on minnow imitations. This group has sharp dorsal-fin spines and sharp, serrated gill-plate bones, so handle them with care. The smaller three members, the white bass, white perch, and yellow bass, are considered panfish and excellent eating.

STRIPED BASS (Morone saxatilis) are primarily an anadronmous fish, native to the East Coast, transplanted to the West Coast, and now transplanted into larger southern and midwestern reservoirs, canals, and rivers. They have a shape similar to that of bass but are silvery, with seven or eight thin but vivid lateral black striped lines on each side. The striper averages about six pounds and often exceeds thirty. Larger and heavier fly tackle is needed for them. They will hit surface and subsurface minnow and eel imitations very well. Night fishing is particularly effective.

Stripers and the others of this group prefer open and deeper water than bass. They are most frequently caught on flies where they enter shallow areas or surface feed on minnows below dams or off long lake points or shallow bay flats. They generally avoid heavy aquatic vegetation.

WHITE BASS (Morone chrysops) also called sand bass, look and act like fat striped bass; but they are much smaller, averaging about one pound and growing only to three or four pounds. They are abundant and widespread in larger lakes, reservoirs, and large river systems. They are principally minnow and insect feeders and strike most smaller surface and subsurface flies that imitate minnows. They are active night and daytime feeders.

WHITE PERCH (Morone americana) are not perch but a bass, and strongly resemble the white bass in shape, color, and size; they do not have the eight or ten dark narrow stripes on their side that white bass have. White perch are primarily located on the upper East Coast states over to the Great Lakes. They strike slow-moving subsurface flies primarily, especially those that imitate small minnows, insects, worms, and crayfish.

YELLOW BASS (Morone mississippiensis) also called brassy bass, are close relatives of the white bass but more gold or yellow in coloration and far more limited in their range. Yellow bass occur naturally in Minnesota, Wisconsin, Michigan, then southward to the Tennessee River drainage in Alabama. The yellow bass will take slow-moving bass flies that imitate small minnows, worms, and insects.

PERCH FAMILY (Percidae). Three members of this family—the yellow perch, walleye, and sauger—are frequently caught by bass fly fishers when using slow-moving subsurface flies, especially minnows, leeches, and insect imitations. All are beautiful fish, but moderate fighters that don't jump; they are all among the finest-eating freshwater fish. Perch are widely distributed and often transplanted to improve fishing; all live well in streams and lakes, preferring cooler water than bass, and deeper and more open water, with sand, gravel, rubble, and ledge-type structure, three to thirty feet deep.

Yellow perch

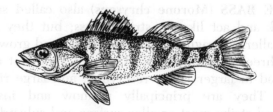

YELLOW PERCH (Perca flavescens) also called ringed perch, is a widely distributed panfish found from about the central United States north. It has a moderately elongated body with vivid olive and golden-olive

back and side-bar patterns with yellow or white belly and bright-orange pectoral and pelvic fins. It has two large separate dorsal fins. Yellow perch average about eight inches, will frequently grow to one or two pounds, and seldom exceed four pounds. They will strike small, slow-moving subsurface swimming and jigging flies best, especially if they are scented or tipped with a piece of red worm. Their strike is delicate.

WALLEYE (Stizostedion vitreum vitreum) also called walleyed pike, are the largest of the perch; they average about 1½ pounds but can exceed 20 pounds. The walleye's most noteworthy feature is its large, glassy, opaque eyes, which allow it excellent deep-water or nighttime vision. Walleyes will strike deep slow-moving subsurface bass flies, especially those that imitate minnows, leeches, and worms. You will catch walleyes on surface, surface-diving, and swimming flies on dark days and at night. In most cases, their strike will be very delicate and their fight less than spectacular.

SAUGER (Stizostedion canadense) or jack salmon are a smaller duplicate of the walleye with more vivid gold and black markings. They average about ¾ pound and frequently reach three or four pounds but seldom exceed seven. Sauger prefer streams, tailwaters, and large lakes. Their range is primarily the Great Lakes, Mississippi River, Ohio River, and Tennessee River drainage.

Note: Perch have a distinctive sandpaper-like feel to their scaled bodies. All three have sharp-spined dorsal fins and sharp gill-plate bones. Sauger and walleye have long, sharp canine-like teeth that should also be avoided—though these teeth do not usually cut your leader like those of a true pike.

Channel catfish

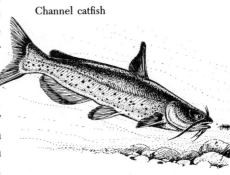

CATFISH (Icturidae) cohabite nearly every stream, pond, and lake you will fly fish for bass. They are easily identified by their whiskers and scaleless skin. Catfish feed primarily by scent; they often feed at night, on both the surface and bottom. Bullheads, channel, blue, and flathead catfish will strike bass flies, especially if you fly fish at night or use scented flies. They are strong, deep fighters. Catfish have small teeth similar to those of bass but strong jaws that can give your fingers a bruising bite. Beware of the sharp, barbed, toxic, spined dorsal and pectoral fins, especially on the smaller catfish. Catfish are superb for eating.

GAR (Lepisosteidae) are an ancient group of predaceous fish, shaped like northern pike and pickerel, with long, bony, heavily toothed snouts or bills. Their scales are large, bony, and armor-plated. Gar inhabit most major warm and cool-water lakes and rivers east of the Rocky Mountains; they are especially abundant in the Midwest and South.

At times, gar will aggressively strike bass flies—especially those that imitate minnows. However, they are

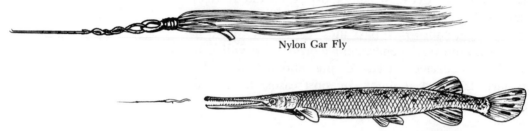

Nylon Gar Fly

Long-nose (or needle-nose) gar

extremely difficult to hook because a hook can seldom penetrate their hard snouts. Occasionally, if they take the fly deep, it will hook in the corners of the mouth behind their snouts. You can better catch gar on fine nylon hair streamers that have no hooks. The nylon hair simply acts like dental floss, tangling between and around their teeth and snouts. They are rather large and slow moving but if intimidated with heavy fly-tackle pressure will fight well and frequently jump. *Never pick a gar up by the mouth or allow one to hit you with its snout or you will be badly cut.* Use a wire bite tippet if you intentionally pursue large gar.

BOWFIN (DOGFISH, GRINDLE) (Amia calva) are a primitive fish with a strong wide snout, dark-olive body and long dorsal fin. They have one or more large black spots at the base of their tail. Bowfin average about four pounds and can grow to twenty. They inhabit bass waters, especially slow rivers, swamps, bayous, canals, and shallow lakes along the Mississippi River drainage, St. Lawrence River, and south to Texas and Florida. They prefer one to four feet of water with heavy surface

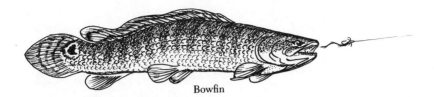

Bowfin

and subsurface aquatic vegetation. They eat minnows, suckers, and panfish and will strike slow-moving subsurface and jigging flies. The bowfin puts up a long, stubborn, powerful fight, nearly always making you think you have hooked a record bass. Since the bowfin has a large, strong-jawed mouth full of long sharp teeth, it's best to use a bite tippet and to keep your fingers far from its mouth.

Note: In addition to these fish, such fish as chub, carp, fallfish, snook, shiners, shad, golden eye, trout, salmon, and char sometimes live in bass waters and will also strike bass flies.

There are many well-illustrated books available on these and other gamefish. A. J. McClane's *Field Guide to Freshwater Fishes* is an excellent, compact handbook with accurate color pictures of each fish and an easy-to-read text.

Fish of all species will vary in color and shape due to their size, sex, age, condition, time of year, and environment. Each has unique characteristics, however, and you should know these. Then, when you catch such fish, you will know how to identify and handle each; and you can then determine what legally you can do with each.

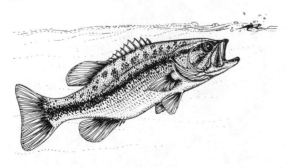

10
The Years Ahead

Once you have learned the basics of bass fly fishing you are ready to reap the rewards. You will find that this method will greatly multiply your pleasure on the water; you will enjoy the process of casting and you will enjoy the special thrill of tempting a really difficult fish to your fly—perhaps a fly you have tied yourself.

It won't all be easy. You can't learn all of bass fly fishing in a week or from any book, magazine, tape, or fly fishing school, but each helps. Skill takes motivation and practice. You'll have to be patient with your flaws and try steadily to correct them. There will be frustrations—wind knots, sloppy casts, the inability to match a specific hatch of insects when fish are rising to them everywhere in sight. You must *want* to perfect your techniques and you must practice constantly. It's worth the effort.

For fly fishing can provide a lifetime of pleasure— and part of that pleasure lies in improving your skills, becoming more adept at the various arts of fly fishing, gaining more and more experience on the water.

Of course the future of *your* fly fishing depends in part upon the future of everyone's fly fishing—and that depends upon the protection of our quarry and of the waters in which they live. Through education and enlightenment, more and more people are coming to love the *quality* of their fishing. They want to fish for wild fish in clean, natural surroundings. Bass and many associated species are plentiful and excellent eating *but* fewer people are killing their fish today. They realize that tempting a fish to a fly and playing it on balanced fly tackle is not only the best part of fishing but also that it provides fish to tempt another day. Sections of lakes and many rivers are now under "catch and release" or "special size" restrictions and the quality of fishing they provide has improved immensely. Carefully releasing most or all of your catch makes good sense.

Bass in most waters are an important link in the food chain's health and balance. They keep many lesser fish and themselves in balance with the ecosystem. If you consistently remove too many adult bass, especially during spawning season, this can drastically curtail bass reproduction and encourage overpopulation of lesser forage fish. If you want to eat bass you catch, keep the smallest legal-length fish. The various panfish that co-inhabit bass waters are abundant and aggressive fly strikers. These fish directly compete with bass and taking sensible numbers of them to eat actually helps provide better bass fly fishing.

As you share bass waters with other fishermen, give them the respect and privacy you expect and appreciate. Be considerate. Don't crowd into their area or disturb their water with your person or boating equipment. If the area is restricted in size, and you need to pass another fisherman on foot or by boat, do so as slowly and quietly as possible, so as not to scare fish or disrupt your fellow angler's mood or concentration. Also, try your best to leave the area you've fished in the same or better condition than when you arrived. Clear up your own litter and any other that is practical to clean up, too. Clean areas attract less litter than those that have litter present.

Because a lot of serious fly fishers have worked hard to protect our waters, the future of fly fishing is bright today. But you will have to help if it is to remain so. Keep improving your skills; keep trying to catch more and more species of fish on the fly; help protect our fisheries; and have lots of fun fly fishing for bass.

Selected Bibliography

BOOKS ON FLY TYING OF INTEREST TO BASS FLY-TYERS

Most Important

Art Flick's Master Fly-Tying Guide by Art Flick et al

Flies (new edition) by J. Edson Leonard

Fly-Tying Materials by Eric Leiser

Universal Fly-Tying Guide by Dick Stewart (excellent for beginners)

Excellent

American Nymph Fly-Tying Manual by Randall Kaufmann

The Fly-Tyer's Almanac, edited by Robert Boyle and Dave Whitlock

Popular Fly Patterns by Terry Hellekson

Saltwater Flies by Kenneth Bay

The Second Fly-Tyer's Almanac, edited by Robert Boyle and Dave Whitlock

Good

The Complete Book of Fly Tying by Eric Leiser

Dick Surrette's Fly Index by Dick Surrette

Flytying and Fly Fishing for Bass and Panfish by Tom Nixon

Modern Dressings for the Practical Angler by Poul Jorgensen

Streamers and Bucktails by Joseph D. Bates, Jr.

Tying and Fishing the Fuzzy Nymphs by Polly Rosborough

Tying and Fishing Terrestrials by Gerald Almy

BOOKS IMPORTANT TO THE BASS FLY FISHERMAN

Most Important

Dave Whitlock's Guide to Aquatic Trout Foods by Dave Whitlock

Fly Fishing in Salt Water by Lefty Kreh

The Masters on the Dry Fly, edited by J. Michael Migel

The Masters on the Nymph, edited by J. Michael Migel and Leonard M. Wright, Jr.

Fly Fishing for Smallmouth Bass by Harry Murray

Excellent

Fishing the Dry Fly as a Living Insect by *Leonard M. Wright, Jr.*

Fly Casting with Lefty Kreh by *Lefty Kreh*

Fly-Fishing Strategy by *Doug Swisher and Carl Richards*

Lamar Underwood's Bass Almanac

Naturals by *Gary Borger*

Through the Fish's Eye by *Mark Sosin and John Clark*

In Fisherman's *"Masterpiece Series" (5 books)*

PERIODICALS OF SIGNIFICANT VALUE TO THE BASS FLY FISHER

Angler Magazine, Box 12155, Oakland, CA 94604
Regular features on western saltwater fly fishing and fly tying

American Angler and Fly Tyer, P.O. Box 280, Intervale, NH 03845
Excellent up-to-date source on tying bass flies plus all other flies—with articles on how to fish them.

BassMaster Magazine, P.O. Box 17116, Montgomery, AL 36141
Excellent feature articles on all phases of bass fishing.

The Flyfisher, P.O. Box 1088, West Yellowstone, MT 59758
The official magazine of the Federation of Fly Fishers (FFF), published quarterly. Membership to FFF includes subscription to the magazine.

Flyfishing, P.O. Box 02112, Portland, OR
97202
Features fly fishing and fly tying

Fly Fisherman, Box 8200, Harrisburg, PA
17105
Features articles on fly fishing and fly tying
throughout the world.

The In-Fisherman, P.O. Box 999, Brainerd,
MN 56401
A superb fishing magazine on all freshwater
gamefish, with excellent fly-fishing features
for bass and associated species.

Rod and Reel, P.O. Box 679, Camden, ME
04873
Interesting fly-fishing articles.

The Roundtable, United Fly Tyers, Inc.,
P.O. Box 723, Boston, MA 02102
Membership in United Fly Tyers, a nonprofit
organization, includes subscription. Articles
on fly tying with how-to instruction.

"Scientific Anglers' Handbooks," 3M Building,
St. Paul, MN 55101
Annual handbooks on general fly fishing, bass
fly fishing, panfish fly fishing, and saltwater
fly fishing.

MAJOR FLY-FISHING ORGANIZATIONS

Federation of Fly Fishermen, P.O. Box 1088,
West Yellowstone, MT 59758
The federation has over 200 clubs nationally,
conducting all types of fly fishing, fly tying,
and conservation activities. With
membership you receive *The Flyfisher*
magazine.

Trout Unlimited, P.O. Box 6225, Bend, OR
97708
Trout Unlimited has chapters throughout the
United States and Canada. It has trout and
salmon fishing and conservation activities.
Local chapters are active in fly-fishing and
fly-tying seminars. With membership you
receive *Trout* magazine.

United Fly Tyers, Inc., P.O. Box 723, Boston,
MA 02102
Active in all types of fly tying and fly-tying
promotion and instruction. Has excellent
magazine, *The Roundtable*, on fly tying.

Saltwater Fly Rodders of America, P.O. Box
304, Cape May Court House, NJ 08120
Active in all types of saltwater fly fishing and
fly tying. Also has magazine with
membership.

BASS FLY-FISHING-RELATED VIDEO TAPES

These tapes are available for sale or rent from L. L.
Bean Customer Service Department and from numerous fly-fishing specialty stores and mail-order catalogs
throughout the United States and Canada.

Fly Fishing for Bass with Dave Whitlock
L.L. Bean's Introduction to Fly Fishing with
Dave Whitlock
Big Mouth by Glen Lau and 3M/Scientific
Anglers
The Essence of Fly Casting by Mel Kreiger
Fly Casting with Lefty Kreh by Lefty Kreh
Smallmouth Bass by Glen Lau

Glossary

Action—A word that expresses the flexibility and power of a fly rod.

AFTMA—American Fishing Tackle Manufacturers Association. American fishing-tackle manufacturers organized to maintain standards of fishing tackle, public information, product quality, marketing, and conservation of the resource.

Animation—The act of making an artificial fly move and act alive.

Aquatic food—Fish foods that are solely aquatic in their origin.

Aquatic insects—Those insects that live some part of their normal life cycle beneath the water.

Arbor—The spindle of a fly-reel spool that the backing line is attached to and wound on.

Attracter (color)—Unnaturally bright color in a fly pattern.

Backing (braided)—A line most commonly composed of several filaments of either nylon or Dacron braided into a single component. Used to extend fly line's length.

Baitcasting—A weighted-artificial-lure casting method thath uses a revolving-spool casting reel called a baitcasting reel.

Bait fish—Various species of small or young fish that other fish regularly eat.

Bank—The higher and steeper sides above a lake or stream, usually created by water cutting or eroding the shoreline.

Bar—A mounded structure in streams and some lakes caused by accumulation of rock, sand, sediment, and dead vegetation, usually protruding out of the water or very near the surfac.

Barb (hook)—The raised cut section of a hook immediately behind the point. It prevents hook from coming out of the fish's mouth.

Barbless hook—A fly hook without a barb.

Bass—A general descriptive term for a group of larger freshwater sunfish, particularly largemouth bass, smallmouth bass, and Kentucky or spotted bass.

Bassbug—A floating fly used for bass fly-fishing.

Beaching—A method of landing a fish by coaxing or forcing it to swim or drift itself aground in the shallow water of a lake or stream shoreline.

Beaver pond—A small lake, usually less than two acres, which has been formed by the damming of small brook or stream by beavers.

Belly—The larger midsection of a fly line. Also may refer to the curve of a fly-line midsection when wind or current pushes it into a C shape.

Bite—A term often used by fly fishers to describe the strike of a fish. Bite also may refer to the distance from hook point and the extent of the bend.

Brackish water—Water that has less salt content than true ocean salt water. Occurs most commonly where freshwater streams meet or mix with saltwater bays and estuaries.

Breakoff—The accidental or purposeful breaking of the leader tipped from a hooked fish—freeing it.

Bream—A general term or name referring to sunfish, especially bluegill, redear, and copper-nose bream.

Brush—Small trees or tree limbs in streams or lakes.

Bubble chain—The string of bubbles that are emitted from a fly when it dives beneath the surface.

Bucktail—A streamer fly constructed from the hair of a deer's tail (bucktail).

Bug—Usually refers to a floating bass fly that might imitate various large insects, frogs, mice, and so on.

Buttcap—The end of a fly-rod handle used for resting and protecting the fly rod and fly reel when stored upright. At times it is rested against the fly fisher's stomach when fighting a large fish.

Canal—A manmade, water-filled ditch used to join lakes or swamps to rivers, or to straighten and quicken the flow of a stream's runoff.

Cast—The act of delivering the fly to the fishing area with fly-rod line and leader. Cast is also used as a descriptive term by the English fly fisher to denote the fly leader.

Catch and release—An expression for catching fish, with immediate release alive and unharmed.

Channel—The main depression caused by flowing water (current).

Char—A group of popular freshwater fish that includes brook trout, lake trout, arctic char, and Dolly Varden.

Chumline—A series of fish food pieces put into the water to attract and congregate hungry fish in a specific area near the fisherman.

Chunk rock—A type of lake or stream shoreline that is made up of rock rubble from apple to watermelon size. Chunk rock is usually excellent structure for bass foods and bass.

Click drag—A simple light-drag system that makes a clicking sound as a metal triangle-shaped paw slips over the reel spool gear.

Clippers—A small tool used to cut and trim the fly line, leader, or tippet material.

Cold-water fish—Fish that thrive best in water temperature ranges from 40° to 60°. For example: trout, char, grayling, and salmon.

Cool-water fish—Fish that thrive best in water temperature ranges from 55° to 70°. For example: smallmouth bass, shad, walleyes, Northern pike, whitefish, striped bass.

Coontail moss—A common and important aquatic plant whose stems and leaves resemble a cat's or coon's tail.

Corkers—Rubber sandals with sharp hard-metal cleats in their soles that are worn over waders, boots, or shoes to increase grip or traction on very slippery rock stream bottoms.

Cork rings—Rings of cork that are glued together and shaped to form the fly-rod handle.

Cove—A small water indenetation in the shoreline of a lake or ocean.

Cover—Some objects above, on, or under the water a bass can get under for comfort and safety.

Crab—A spiderlike crustacean that bass often eat when living in brackish water.

Crayfish—A freshwater lobsterlike small crustacean very popular as fish food.

Creel—A container cooled by water evaporation used to keep and carry dead fish.

Crossbar (fly reel)—A part of a fly-reel frame that is chiefly for structural support between the two sides. Sometimes referred to as a post.

Cruising (fish)—An expression describing a fish that is moving about in lake or stream in order to find food.

Crustacea—An important group of fresh- and salt-water aquatic invertebrates which are fed upon by many fish. Shrimp, scud, sowbugs, crabs, and crayfish are examples.

Current—The flowing or gravitational pull of water in a stream. Lakes and oceans also have currents.

Deaddrift—The drift of a fly downstream without action other than what is given it by the natural current flow. It means no drag.

Deer hair—Body hair, usually coarse and semi-hollow, from various deer. Used for tying many fly designs and patterns.

Density—Refers to the weight of fly line, leader, or fly compared to theweight of the water. *High density* means much heavier than water and fast sinking. *Low density* means slow sinking or even floating.

Dipnet—The device used to scoop up and hold a hooked fish. Also called a landing net.

Dise drag—An intricate, highly efficient type of fly-reel brake or drag system that employs a disc or shoe arrangement similar to a car's disc brake.

Dorsal fin—The top or back fin of a fish.

Double hook—A fly-hook design that has two points, barbs, and bends, and one common shank. Most commonly used for making Atlantic salmon flies.

Drag (guides)—The rod's guides and fly line create points of friction that are often referred to as drag.

Drag (line)—An expressive term used to describe a current or wind pull on the fly line that results in pulling the fly unnaturally over or through the water.

Drag (reel)—A part of the fly reel that adjusts the spool's tension when line is pulled off the reel by the fly fisher or a fish.

Dress—The application of waterproofing or flotant material to the fly line, leader, or fly.

Drift—Describes the path a fly travels while it is fished down the stream's current.

Drop off—An abrupt or sharp increase in water depth that is often an ideal area in which bass congregate.

Dropper fly—One or more flies tied to the fly leader or dropped off the main fly tied to the leader.

Dry fly—A basic fly design that floats on the water's surface. It is usually made of low density, waterproof materials to hold in the water's surface film.

Dry-fly paste—A paste compound used to waterproof the water-absorbent materials of floating flies.

Dry-fly spray—Aerosol spray compound used to

waterproof the water-absorbent materials of a dry fly.

Dubbing—A fly-tying material consisting of natural hairs and/or synthetic fibers blended into a loose felt and used to form the body of many floating and sinking flies.

Eddy—A calm, slowly swirling (upstream) water flow in a stream behind an obstruction such as a boulder, log, bar, or moss bed.

Extension butt—A one to six-inch handle-like extension below the fly rod's reel seat, used mainly for better leverage when forcing or fighting a large fish. The butt end is placed against your stomach or forearm for extra leverage.

Feedinig—A fish's eating or striking period.

Fighting—The act of tiring a hooked fish in preparation of landing it.

Fighting butt—See "extension butt."

Fingerling—A general descriptive term used to describe various larger fish species (trout, bass, catfish, etc.) when they are about finger-length in size.

Fishery—A body of water that sustains a healthy fish population and has potential for fly-fishing success.

Fish for fun—Catching and immediately releasing fish alive and unharmed. Usually it is illegal to keep or kill fish caught in these designated areas.

Fishing vest—A vest with assorted pockets for carrying the various flies, reels, and accessories used while walking, wading, or fly-fishing.

Fish scent—An odor placed on an artificial lure to give it a fish-attracting odor.

Flat—A wide shallow-water section of a lake, stream, or ocean. Flats usually have a relatively uniform smooth surface.

Flotant—Material used to waterproof fly lines, leaders, and flies.

Fly—The artificial lure used in fly-fishing.

Fly design—Describes type of fly or purpose of fly.

Fly-line finish—The smooth outermost coating of the fly line.

Fly pattern—The color and material makeup of a particular fly design.

Fly-tackle balance—Each component of fly tackle being matched to perform correctly.

Fly tier—A person who makes or "ties" flies for fly-fishing.

Forage fish—Various species of small or young fish that other fish regularly eat.

Freshwater—Water with little or no salt content. It also refers to fish species that are adapted only to freshwater environs.

Fry—The first stage of development of a fish after hatching from the egg or live birth. Usually from one-half to two inches in length.

Gaff—A hook-and-handle tool used to hook and capture larger fish. Also refers to the act of hooking and capturing a fish once it has been tired with rod and reel.

Gamefish—A general term used to denote those species of fish that will readily strike or attack an artificial lure or fly. Also deals with the ability and willingness of the fish to fight very hard after it is hooked.

Gap—The distance between the hook shank and the point.

Gill—The respiratory organ of a water-breathing fish, located just behind the head.

Gill plate—A bony structure on the cheek or side of bass and other fish. Some fish, such as walleye and snook, have sharp or sharp serrated edges on their gill plates that may cut leader or hands.

Giving butt—Using the fly-rod butt section to slow or stop a hard-fighting fish's swim.

Giving tip—Holding the rod tip forward and high to provide maximum shock absorption to prevent the leader's tippet from breaking and the fly from being pulled out of the fish's mouth.

Grab—A term often used to describe a brief period fish go through when they are willing to strike a fly.

Grain—The unit of measurement used for calibrating fly-line weights.

Grease—The application of paste to line or fly dressing to enhance flotation.

Greased line—A floating line that has been coated with a paste flotant to enhance flotability and mending ease.

Green trout—A common name for largemouth bass.

Grip—Another name for the handle of a fly rod.

Hackle—Usually neck and back feathers of a chicken, however, can also be from other chickenlike birds such as grouse or partridge.

Hairbug—A bass surface fly whose head and body are constructed with bouyant body hair from a deer, elk, caribou, or antelope.

Handle (reel)—A brank on a fly-reel spool used for reeling the fly line on to the fly reel.

Handle (rod)—The grip used for holding the fly rod while casting, fishing, and fighting a fish.

Hauling—A method of increasing fly-line speed during pickup, back, or forward casting. It is accomplished by hand pulling on the fly line between the rod's stripper guide and the fly reel.

Hold—A place where a fish such as salmon, trout, or bass will rest or remain stationary for a period of time.

Holding fish—Describes a fish that remains in a particular spot in a lake or stream.

Honey hole—An expression used by bass fishermen, meaning a favorite or very good location where big or lots of bass congregate.

Hook barb—The raised metal slice off the hook's point and bend. The barb helps prevent the hook from backing out of the fish's mouth tissue.

Hook bend—The curved or bent section just behind the hook shank.

Hook eye—The closed loop part of a fly hook to which the leader tip or tippet is attached.

Hook (fly)—The device used to hold a fish that strikes or attempts to eat the fly.

Hook (-ing) fish—Setting the hook in a fish's mouth tissue after the fish has struck.

Hookkeeper—The small clip or eyelet at the front of the fly-rod handle used to store the fly when not in use.

Hook point—The needlelike point on the end of the hook's bend. It enhances faster penetration into the fish's mouth tissue.

Hook shank—The length of fly hook exclusive of its eye and bend. Generally it is the section to which the fly materials are tied.

Hook size—The distance or amount of gap on a fly hook or fly. Also refers to the overall length and size of wire the hook is made from. Generally hook sizes range from largest #5/0 to smallest #36.

Jack salmon—A common name for a sauger or walleye pike.

Jump—When a hooked fish comes up out of the water in an attempt to shake the hook or break the leader.

Knotless—A leader that has no knots tied in it to join different-size sections or tippet.

Land (-ing)—Capturing a hooked fish after it has been tired.

Leader—The transparent part of the fly-fishing linje between the fly line and fly. It may include tippet section.

Leader straightener—A rubber or leather pad used to heat and straighten the coils from a leader.

Leader wallet—A convenient pocketed container for storage of extra leaders to be carried while fly-fishing.

Ledge—An exposed or underwater sheer rock (shale, granite, limestone) formation like a wall that provides excellent structure for bass.

Leech—A bloodsucking, wormlike aquatic invertebrate or a fly imitating it.

Levels—The amount of water or depth of a stream or lake.

Line—Short expression for fly line. When the fly line scares a fish it is commonly referred to as lining it.

Line drag—The resistances a fly line may incur as it moves through the fly-rod guides, air, or water.

Line guard—The part of a fly reel that the fly line passes through or over as it is wound on or off the reel spool. It acts as a guide and reduces wear from line friction.

Lip a bass—Grasping the lower lip of a bass with your hand to land it.

Loop—The general term describing the U shape of the fly as it unrolls forward or backward during the casting cycle.

Loop to loop—An expression used to describe the joining of fly line to leader, leader to tippet, where a closed loop in each is joined to make the other connection.

Lure—An imitation fish food with one or more hooks on it. As a verb it refers to attracting a fish to strike a fly.

Magnum butt—An extra-strong butt section.

Manipulate—Generally refers to more intricate fly presentation and actions accomplished with fly rods of nine feet or longer.

Matuka—Generally refers to a special fly design in which feathers are uniquely wrapped to the length of a hook shank and/or body of a fly so that they appear as part of the body. The word *Matuka* originated from a bird, the matukar, whose feathers were popularly used for this type of fly.

Mending—The act of lifting or rolling the fly line with the rod to reposition it in order to avoid fly drag due to current speeds or wind.

Mesh—The net bag or seine of a dip net or landing net.

Milfoil—A common and important aquatic plant.

Minnow—A general term used for many species of smaller fishes (one- to eight-inches long), as well as the same size of immature larger fish.

Monofilament—A single filament or strand of nylon used for fishing line, leader or tippet materials.

Moss bed—A large underwater growth of aquatic plants.

Mudding—The term used to describe a fish stirring up a visible cloud of mud or silt as it feeds and swims on the bottom.

Muddler—A very popular and effective type of artificial fly that has a large clipped deer-hair head and usually incorporates hair and feathers for its wings.

Neck—A long narrow body of water usually found at stream's inlet to a lake.

Net—Refers to the act of landing a fish with a dipnet or landing net.

Neutral color—Color and pattern of a fly or natural food that does not contrast with its surroundings.

No-kill—A fishery policy of catching and releasing unharmed live fish.

Nongamefish—A general term used to describe those species of fish that never or seldom strike or attack artificial lures or flies.

Nymph—Refers to the water-breathing or immature stage of aquatic insects. Also a fly that imitates these insects.

Nymphing—Fly-fishing with aquatic nymph imitations. A term used to describe a fish that is foraging for aquatic nymphs.

On the reel—Fighting a fish by using the fly reel to give or take in fly line.

Outlet—That part of a lake where water flows out.

Palming the reel—The application of a palm against the fly-reel outer spool flange to add extra drag pressure on a fish pulling line off the fly reel.

Panfish—A large group of abundant freshwater gamefish species, generally under two pounds in weight. Included are sunfish, bluegill, yellow perch, white bass, crappie, etc.

Pencil popper—A long, slender, hard-head bass bug.

Perch—A group of fish including the yellow perch, white perch, darters, and walleyed pike.

Pickup—The lifting of a fly line, leader, and fly off the water as the backcast is begun.

Pike—A group of cold and cool freshwater gamefish including Northern pike, pickerel, and muskie. Sometimes walleyed pike (which is not a true pike but a perch) is included.

Pocket—Usually refers to a small surface or underwater area surrounded by a structure.

Pocket water—A series of bottom depressions or pockets in a stream riffle or run section.

Point—Refers to the narrow, pointed section of land that juts out into a lake or stream.

Polaroids—A popular term for sunglasses that polarize or filter out certain angles of light rays. They reduce reflective sunlight off water so fish are more easily seen beneath.

Pond—Usually refers to a small lake less than five acres in surface, except in Maine, where it is often used interchangeably with lake.

Popping bug—A topwater or surface bass but that because of its head shape makes an audible "pop" on the water surface when it is briskly twitched or jerked.

Pound test—Refers to the strength of a fishing line, leader, or tippet. Sometimes called breaking strength or test.

Power (casting)—Generally describes the wrist and arm movement used to energize the fly rod during the power stroke to cast the fly line, leader, and fly.

Power (rod)—The degree of efficiency a rod has in casting, hooking, and fishing a fish.

Predator fish—A fish that eats live fish, insects, and other animals.

Presentation—The placement of the fly on or below the water. Also describes the fly's path and action on the water.

Pressure (rod)—How hard a fly fisher pulls, restricts, or fights a hooked fish with the fly rod, reel, and leader determines the amount of pressure being used.

Pumping a fish—Pulling a large fish by using a pumping or rod-butt-lifting action as the fish sounds or pulls away. As the rod is quickly

lowered after the pump-up, the reel takes up the line gained on the fish.

Pupa—Generally refers to stage between larva and adult of the caddis and midge aquatic insects. Also common descriptive term used for the artificial fly imitation of the same insects.

Put and take—A fishery management policy that involves artificial stocking of catchable fish and encouragement of killing and removing these fish when caught.

Putting down—Fish that have been scared by the flyfisher and stop feeding have been *put down*.

Rapids—A section of stream that has a high gradient and fast, rough-surfaced flowing water.

Reading water—Visually examining the surface of the water to evaluate fishing potential, depth, and fish location.

Reel—To wind in or retrieve the fly line, leader, backing, etc. Also short expression for fly reel.

Reel hand—The hand and arm used to hold or reel in the fly line. Same as line hand.

Reel saddle—The part of a reel that provides means for attaching the reel to the rod seat and/or handle.

Reel seat—The part of a fly rod, just behind the rod handle, where the fly reel is fastened.

Reel spool—The part of a fly reel where the line is wound and stored.

Riffle—The section of a stream where the water flows shallowly and rapidly over an irregular bottom so that the surface riffles. Also refers to a water surface slightly disturbed by the wind.

Rim drag—A method of providing fly-reel drag resistance against a fighting fish by applying finger or hand pressure to the rim of the fly reel's spool.

Rising fish—A fish that is visibly feeding just below or at the water's surface.

Rod blank—A fly rod before it is fitted with guides and handle or other finished fly-rod accessories.

Rod guides—Also **Fly-rod guides**, the closed loop structures fastened to the fly-rod shaft that hold the fly line on the rod's length.

Roll—The movement of a fish when it arches up and down from the surface as it feeds.

Run—The fleeing swim a fish makes when it has been hooked and frightened. Also describes a stretch of stream just below a riffle and above the pool.

Saltwater—A general term used to describe the fish or fishing in salty oceans, seas, and other similar saltwater areas.

Saltwater fly—An artificial fly that is made principally to be fished in salt water. Its hook must resist salt corrosion.

School—A group of same species of fish swimming together.

Scud—A small shrimplike crustacean or a fly imitating it.

Selective—Refers to the feeding habits of fish

preferring special flies or special presentation of flies.

Shade line—A water area sheltered from direct light, creating a shadow area. A shade line can be created by a single tree or a mountain but predator fish usually prefer this low-light-intensity area to brighter areas.

Shell cracker—A common name for the redear sunfish.

Shoal—A shallow-bottom area in a lake or stream or estuary.

Shoot(-ing)—A term referring to the fly line or shooting line that is pulled out from the force or momentum of the casting power and extended fly line weight.

Shoreline—The area immediately adjacent to the water's edge, along lakes and streams.

Shrimp—A widely distributed, important crustaceanand also its fly imitation.

Skater—A design of floating fly that has a very long hackle or hair around the hook to enable it to sit high or skate across the water's surface.

Slack line—When the fly line has little or no tension on it between the fly reel, rod, and the fly.

Slough—A sluggish or nonflowing, narrow, blind-end body of water usually created by a stream changing to a new path or channel. The old channel becomes a slough if water still connects it to the stream.

Snagguard—A device on a fly that prevents the fly hook from snagging or hanging on various obstacles (rocks, logs, moss, etc.) near or in the fishing water.

Snake guide—A simple two-footed, open wire loop fly-rod guide, designed principally to reduce friction and overall weight and hold the fly line close to the fly-rod shaft. It slightly resembles a semicoiled snake in shape.

Snelled fly—An artificial fly with a short permanent section of gut or monofilament attached to it. On the opposite end is a fixed closed loop to attach the snell to the leader.

Spawn—The act of fish reproduction. Also refers to a mass of fish eggs.

Spawning—The act of reproduction between male (cock) and female (hen) fish.

Spawning runs—The movement of fish or a number of fish from their resident water to a more suitable area to mate and to lay their eggs.

Spillway—The outlet section of a lake where the water flows over a particular section of the dam.

Spin-casting—A method of casting weighted artificial lures that utilize a spin-cast reel that has a push-button arrangement to release the casting line from a stationary reel spool. Line spins off the reel with the pull of the weighted lure.

Spinning—A method of lure-casting that utilizes a fixed-spool casting reel in which the line spins off as the weighted casting lure pulls it out.

Spin-rayed fin—A stiff sharp-pointed fin ray or group of fish with this type of fin.

Splice—The joining of two fly-line sections together.

Spook—Scare a fish so much that it stops feeding or swims away and hides.

Spring creek—A stream in which the water originates from the flow of subsurface spring water.

Straightening (fly line or leader)—The removal of coils or twists in the fly line or leader caused by their storage on the fly reel.

Strawberry bass—A common name for a crappie.

Streamer—A subsurface fly that imitates small fish or similarly shaped natural creatures a fish might strike or eat.

Strike—A fish hitting or biting the natural food or artificial fly. The action a fly fisher takes with fly rod and line to set the hook in a fish's mouth.

Stringer—A length of cord, rope, or chain for retaining, keeping alive, and carrying caught fish.

Stripper guide—The first large guide on the butt section of a fly rod above the rod handle. It is designed to reduce friction and enhance line-casting and retrieving.

Stripping—The act of rapidly retrieving a fly and fly line that involves making a series of fast pulls on the fly line with the line hand.

Structure—Describes objects in the water that fish would live near. Used more in lake fishing than in stream fishing.

Studs—Metal protrusions on the soles of wading shoes or boots for improving footing on very slick wet rocks or ice, etc.

Swim—The way a sinking fly moves through the water as it is being fished. It may move like a minnow or a nymph, for example, or simply swim as an attracter.

Synthetic tying materials—Fly-tying materials that are manmade, for example, Orlon, Mylar, and FishHair.

Tackle—A general term covering all equipment used in fly-fishing.

Tag end—The forward end of a leader or tippet.

Tail—The caudal fin of a fish. Also refers to capturing and/or landing a hooked fish by grasping it just in front of its tail. The lower or end (downstream) of a stream pool.

Tailer—A tool for tailing (landing) fish. It has a locking lkoop on the handle that locks around the fish's tail.

Tailing—A term often used to describe a fish feeding in a position along the bottom in shallow water so that its tail sometimes sticks above the surface of the water.

Tailwater—A stream coming from a large man-made dam.

Taker—The fish's action in catching food or a fly.

Taper—The shape of a fly line or leader. May also be used in describing fly-rod shape.

Terrestrial food—Fish foods thath are land-born but have fallen into the water.

Terrestrial insect—Insects that are land-born air breathers. Included are grasshoppers, crickets, ants, beetles, etc.

Tide—The periodic raising and lowering of water levels in streams, lakes, and oceans due to gravitational forces or releases of impounded waters.

Tie—Describes the making of artificial flies. Also term used to describe forming various line, leader, and fly knots.

Tippet—The small end of a leader or additional section of nylon monofilament tied to the end of the leader.

Tip-top—The fly-rod line guide that is fitted over the rod's tip end.

Treble hook—A fish hook with three bends, barbs, and points joined on a common shank.

Trolling—Fishing a fly or lure by pulling it behind a boat. Less commonly, fishing by wading or walking with the fly dragging in the water behind.

Trout—A group of very popular freshwater ganefish that live in cold, pure water. Includes rainbow trout, golden trout, brown trout, cutthroat trout, brook trout, etc.

Twitch—A small movement given to the fly by using the rod tip or a short fly-line strip.

Vest (fishing vest)—A vestlike garment containing a number of various-size pockets used to carry flies and other fishing accessory items while fly-fishing.

Waders—Waterproof combination of shoes and pants used for wading.

Wading—Walking on the bottom of a stream, lake, or ocean in water no deeper than your chest.

Wading shoes—Shoes used over stocking-foot waders for wading.

Wading staff—A walking cane used to assist in wading, particularly on slick, irregular bottoms and in swift water.

Warm-water fish—Fish that thrive best in water temperature ranges from 65° to 85°.

Water clarity—The degree of transparency water has, how far below the surface you can see an object.

Water color—Refers to a water's color tinge. It is affected by suspended particles and the bottom color reflection.

Water condition—A general expression fly fishers use to describe the combination of level, temperature, and clarity.

Water wagon—A term and product name for the foot-paddle boat.

Weedguard—A simple wire or nylon device on a fly that prevents it from hooking vegetation in the fishing area.

Wiggle nymph—A two-section hinge-bodied artificial nymph fly.

Wind knot—A simple but troublesome overhand knot that is accidentally tied on the fly line or leader while casting.

Woolly worm—A design of sinking fly that has a fuzzy or woolly body and hackle spiraled around and over the body's length. Also the larva of terrestrial moths or butterflies.

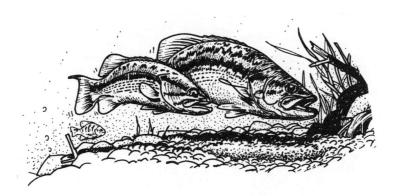